The
Last
Bastion

JENNIFER CHAPMAN

The Last Bastion

Women Priests —
the Case For and Against

Methuen · London

First published in Great Britain 1989
by Methuen London
Michelin House, 81 Fulham Road, London SW3 6RB
Copyright © 1989 Jennifer Chapman

Printed in Great Britain
by Richard Clay Ltd, Bungay, Suffolk

A CIP catalogue record for this book is available
from the British Library

ISBN 0-413-18280-0

FOR

*My parents
Peter
and Pat
Johnson*

Contents

Acknowledgement

I am grateful to The Society of Authors who awarded a grant from The Authors' Foundation/ K. Blundell Trust to assist my research, and to Alex Bennion at Methuen, who initiated and edited this book.

My gratitude is also extended to all who have helped me by agreeing to be interviewed and providing their expert knowledge, with particular thanks to Jeremy Haslam of Royston Library.

Introduction

The ordination of women is one of the most controversial issues facing Britain today. It touches the hearts and consciences of moderate men and women, the middle-class backbone of the country, the Sunday-best people who value family life, fair play and tradition. Nowhere are these values more preciously guarded than within the parish churches, currently attracting larger congregations than have been witnessed in decades as religion worldwide is in revival. And yet the question of women priests threatens to shatter not only individual parish communities, but the Church of England as a whole.

The issue is red hot. Women in tweed suits and sensible shoes have taken to placard-waving outside Church House. Some are for, some against, what they have in common is strength of feeling, their banners the only visible evidence of the soul-searching anguish shared equally by the bishops, the clergy and the laity, who sooner or later must decide.

In the course of my research for this book, I met men and women with every conceivable view on the subject. Some were energetically hostile, even exhibiting hatred of their opponents, while others were weary and sad, fearing the dreaded schism. I met politicians, bishops, priests, deacons, deaconesses and lay people. In Australia I was met at Sydney Airport by the militant MOW (Movement for the Ordination of Women) moderator, Dr Patricia Brennan, who took me to tea at the Hilton and told me she was a media person and a prophet and might go on hunger strike. In America, where Anglican women have been ordained for more than a decade, I met prominent 'breakaway' Anglican, Mrs Auburn Faber Traycik, who talked of 'priestettes' and the moral disintegration of mainstream American Anglicanism, or Episcopalianism.

In a student's room on the Kent University campus I listened to the Bishop of Durham warning that the in-fighting would encourage atheism in the world at large, and express his surprise at being in agreement with anything Mrs Thatcher had to say, following the news that she is an advocate of women's ordination.

I met nuns in favour and nuns against. I talked with embittered women deacons who feel cheated by the Church, hope fading and hardening into cynicism; and women 'against' in the same mood. I listened to an eminent theologian explaining the Scandal of Particularity as she did her ironing. Everyone was more human than, somehow, I had expected, although on one occasion I was foolish enough to suggest to a clergyman that all the theology seemed to be getting in the way of simple faith. Nearly two thousand years of tradition is one of the strongest arguments against ordaining women, although those who oppose the move offer more esoteric objections, even suggesting that women are already more favoured in the eyes of God and that His assignment of the priesthood to men was merely a sop to prevent them from feeling left out.

In late twentieth-century Anglicanism, this is exactly how those against women priests are beginning to feel, left out. It has already happened to traditionalist Anglicans in America, and within the Church of England it remains to be seen how those in favour and those against are going to be able to carry on sitting next to one another in the same pew.

The Bishop of London, and leading opponent, Dr Graham Leonard, has said that those clergy not in favour of women priests should stay on in their churches after the go-ahead is given for women's ordination, when and if it happens, but it is becoming clear that in doing so the Church will be pockmarked with 'no-go areas' for women – dioceses and parishes where the male supremacists will gravitate. Equally, these traditionalist clergy feel they are being passed over for preferment, that their liberal-thinking colleagues already get all the best jobs. 'We are legislating for schism,' says Synod member and government minister, John Selwyn Gummer. But the big change seems to be that the traditionalists are becoming the renegades.

In this book I shall be looking at the history behind the present debate and at how the Christian attitude towards sex over two millennia has kept women out of the Holy Priesthood. I shall also look at the Scandal of Particularity, the idea that it is wrong to represent God in human terms, either male or female, let alone to favour one sex over the other.

In the latter part of the book I shall turn to the General Synod of the Church of England and to the once-a-decade Lambeth Conference, in order to look at the background to the debate there. Then there are the other Churches and religions: Rome, the Nonconformists, the Jews, the Muslims and the Sikhs – how are they treating their women? And the Fundamentalists, the evangelical Christians who are experiencing 'the big revival', their numbers growing faster than anywhere else in the Church; yet here women are neither seeking nor being offered leadership roles. Literal interpretation of Scripture encourages them positively to embrace their subordination to men.

It has to be undeniable that the rise of the women's movement and the renewed stirrings in the Church are in some way related, although there are protagonists on both sides of the debate who attempt to separate the two. The connection is used by traditionalists who argue that what is happening in society has and should have nothing to do with such a fundamental theological question; that the priesthood is a matter of God's will as stated in the Bible. On the other hand, liberal theologians like the Bishop of Durham say that all tradition has come from culture and that it was the nature of society two thousand years ago which dictated an exclusively male priesthood. I met Bishop Jenkins at the 1988 Lambeth Conference, on a day when bishops from the Anglican Communion were trying to reach some sort of compromise over the issue not of women priests, but of women bishops. They had a similar struggle over the question of polygamy and in both instances fundamentalist theology lost out to culture.

Lambeth '88 was, perhaps, the high point of the present debate. Try as the bishops did to play down the women's issue, giving it only a day and a half in the three-week-long conference, it was, and still is, the biggest, longest-running news story the Church has had since the Reformation. The world waited on Lambeth, as if by some miracle all would be resolved and we would know one way or another what was to happen about women's ordination. That it wasn't like that cannot be too surprising; after all, every shade of Anglican opinion was represented in the 500-plus purple-clothed men who had travelled from throughout the world to Canterbury. Yet something of a miracle came out of the Conference. Before it began there was a widely expressed fear that it could be the last one, that disagreement over the issue of women priests and bish-ops could break the Anglican Communion of churches worldwide; but anyone who experienced the atmosphere during those three weeks can understand why they would meet again in 1998, and it was only surprising that they didn't decide to make it sooner.

Lambeth was a miracle of compromise, the bishops agreeing to disagree and setting an example to the rest of the world as to how people who cannot agree don't have to split up and fight. This is not to say that there isn't any in-fighting. Inside the Church of England, just as elsewhere in Anglicanism, in Australia, Africa, still in America, the ordination of women is a harmfully divisive issue, although that doesn't necessarily mean it is wrong.

There is a general assumption that one day women will be ordained priests in the Church of England, but the question that remains is 'when?'. Many people I have spoken to who are in favour no longer believe that it will happen this century; some even think that Rome may get there first. Meanwhile, the Anglican bishops are still agonising over the significance of Eve's creation from Adam's rib.

The people I talked to while researching the book are broadly representative of the many views currently held on why women should or should not be ordained to the priesthood. I have had to be selective; after all, there are now more than a thousand women deacons (deacons are ordained; deaconesses are not), and in the worldwide Anglican Communion a similar number of women priests, all of them pioneers and with a story to tell. And in talking to representatives of other Churches I have been able only to touch on the picture there as this is a book concerned primarily with the present situation in the Church of England, the broadest of the denominations, and with 'a terrible reputation', as the Archbishop of York, Dr John Habgood, told Synod, 'for saying one thing at one stage and then having second thoughts'.

There is still time enough for the re-think, and several stages of deliberation before July 1991, when, assuming that the measures to enable women to become priests have survived diocesan consultation, the General Synod must make its final decision. The matter would then go to Parliament and, if approved, Royal Assent sought in the spring of 1992.

My guess is that it will happen in this time scale, but whether it should, I hesitate to say. The mystery of religion seems to have little to do with what is perceived objectively to be right and wrong. A hundred years from now the debate will probably be lost in time and women as commonplace in the pulpit as anywhere else. The point is that the pulpit will, almost certainly, still be in use.

ONE

Women leading the way

'Most women want to be led. They don't want to be priests.' So says the former Conservative MP Peter Bruinvels, who is a lay member of the General Synod of the Church of England.

His view is representative of a sizeable minority still blocking women's progress in the ministry, but in this first chapter I have begun with the stories of three women and a married couple, who, in their different ways, are trying to disprove the Bruinvels dictum.

'It's absolute rubbish,' cries Sister Denzil, an ordained deacon and member of the Community of St Andrew in London's Notting Hill.

St Andrew's is a unique community of some twenty habited sisters in the Church of England. Eleven of the nuns are ordained deacons and their lives are a combination of pastoral, priestly work and that of the 'religious' (members of contemplative orders), which they share in a small oasis of calm, just around the corner from Westbourne Park tube station, in a house where notices request that doors be closed carefully and quietly.

Sister Denzil, a tall yet fragile-looking figure, nevertheless exhibits considerable spirit at the suggestion that she and the rest of womankind prefer to be led. She is in her sixties, has been with St Andrew's more than thirty years, and is a familiar face outside Church House during Synod sessions, where she can be seen silently holding a placard with the single, poignant word 'Waiting'.

When she took her vows of poverty, chastity and obedience she knew she had not opted for an easy life, but she hadn't reckoned on the hardest part being that of obedience: 'It was far more authoritative years ago but it's still hard, having to be under somebody's rule – we're just not like that – we're all individuals.

'It's difficult to talk about this. When you are called to a religious community, part of that is not always being able to do what you want. Conditioning over thousands of years has caused some women to think that they prefer to be told what to do.

'Very early on I could see no reason why women should not be ordained to the priesthood. A priest is someone who works alongside people but who is also trying to be close to God, to mediate. Ideally, we don't need priests – any person who does God's work, who listens to God and to people, should be able to minister the sacraments. I feel that I am a priest, but male priests feel so threatened if I say that, and men and women feel strange about women being priests. It's the same as it was with women doctors. One woman said to me: "If there are women priests as well, I won't have any men in my life." I can understand that, but there are women against women priests because of a feeling of not wanting other women to "put one over" on them.

'I think more men would come to church if women were priests, just as more women than men do now. Sexuality and spirituality are bound up together. Also, in a sense, it's a weak thing to do to come to church and some men don't like acknowledging this weakness.'

Receiving the Eucharist, the consecrated bread and wine, is not possible for the sisters at St Andrew's unless a man is officiating, and for Sister Denzil this is a cause of great sadness. She thinks carefully when asked whether she also has feelings of anger and frustration, and the answer is 'no', only sadness, although she goes on to say: 'I mind very much. I do actually find it inappropriate that someone has to come in to give the Eucharist. We are a Christian community – we work and pray together – we have the same ethos and yet we can't preside at the central act of worship, although only one other sister feels the same about this as I do.'

There are two men who consecrate the Eucharist for the sisters, the local vicar and his curate. The vicar is a member of the

Movement for the Ordination of Women, the curate is not, yet both men choose not to make even the smallest concession towards equality in the terms sought by Sister Denzil. One aspect of the services the two men conduct which is most hurtful to Sister Denzil is the sexist language, the constant use of terms such as 'Sons of God' and 'mankind'. 'I'm not a son of God, I'm a daughter,' she says.

The issue of 'inclusive language' is, it seems, as controversial as that of women priests, with even those in favour of female ordination disinclined to 'muck about with the words'. Describing the argument put forward by the curate, Sister Denzil says: 'He does not agree with inclusive language, just as he says women cannot be ordained. He points out that if we were able to become priests we could then go on to become bishops, which would put us over men, and St Paul said that man is the head of woman.' This being the case, is the curate right? Sister Denzil points out that Paul said a lot else to contradict such a pronouncement.

Asked why she remains obedient to a system with which she is in fundamental disagreement, why she waits quietly outside Church House in Westminster with a pleading placard rather than a megaphone, why she doesn't just do what she feels and believes to be right — celebrate the Eucharist herself on official ground as opposed to attending private and unrecognised gatherings where the experience has been marvellous — she is both humble and self-effacing: 'I'm tarred with the same brush as the Women Against the Ordination of Women people — I'm against being strident.' And, she feels, with good reason.

Since she began standing outside Church House, when the Synod sits, she has noticed a change. A few years ago, Synod members would smile and acknowledge the 'Waiting' message, wish her well and express the hope that the wait wouldn't be too long: 'There are more stony-faced people around now. I feel there is a backlash. People have been strident and I think it's been counter-productive. I know that sometimes you have to raise your voice and cry, but I'm against being strident.'

'I remember, at the age of six, thinking: I want to be up there by the altar.' The Rev. Ann Easter, ordained deacon in June 1987, one of the first to get this far in the Church of England (women were first ordained deacons in the UK on 27 February 1987), is not looking to be led.

Ann is a tall, striking redhead of indeterminate age: 'I never say how old I am – I think it's wrong to categorise people in this way.' She is the parish worker attached to the combined parishes of St John and St James and Christ Church, Stratford, in the East End of London where she was born and brought up. She is also a high-profile media favourite and has been pictured striding across the pages of the tabloid press in her hand-tailored cassock and stiletto heels, with captions that read 'definitely feminine' and 'pin-up priest'.

Her first memories of the Church go back to when she was three years old and living in Upton Park, close to West Ham football club. She lived in her grandmother's house and it was Gran who took her to church: 'She went to whichever one had the best old-age pensioners' club and outings, and she took me with her to the services. But when it was time for me to start Sunday school my parents heard that there were some rowdy boys at the C. of E. classes, so I got involved in the local Methodist Church, where they were quieter. It was there I remember thinking that I wanted to be up at the altar, where the minister was.'

Ann went on to teach Sunday School herself and attended Bible classes, where she began to realise that the comparative austerity in style of the Nonconformists was not for her. 'There was this minister's wife who taught us that make-up and nail varnish and all that sort of thing was 'of the devil'. This caused me some real heart-searching because I was drawn to the flashy East-Enders' way of dressing. My mother had always been glamorous, so I was really torn. I wanted to experiment with make-up and jewellery and bright dresses.'

It was at this cosmetics crossroads that she re-discovered the Church of England at its most glorious and decorative. Through school, she became involved with the Society of Anglican Friars at Plaistow: 'It was like coming home – all the candles and smells and bells. It was beautiful and what I wanted. I loved the sensuality of it all. I was in love with it.'

When she left school Ann decided on a career in nursing and spent three years at Guys Hospital in London, but she had not found her vocation: 'I wanted to give more than just physical care. I would have been better as the doctor, not the nurse. I saw the illness of the whole person, not just a bad leg, but when I tried to speak to patients I'd be told off, told I wasn't there to talk to people but to get on with my work.'

Ann left nursing to have her first child, and there followed a succession of jobs, including working in a butcher's shop. She wasn't cut out for being a mum at home all day in the confines of a tiny house, but going back to nursing was not her inclination. She thought about accountancy, but not for long, then joined a drama course with the idea of eventually teaching; but the vocation still wasn't there.

'I volunteered to be the church warden at St Philip and St James, Plaistow.'

This was the early 1970s and Ann, still entranced by the Anglo–Catholic world, had yet to question the attitude of the Church when it came to women. She was not turned down for the job as church warden, she was not even considered. St Philip and St James did not have women in the job.

'I felt I really had something to offer. The friars down at Plaistow were lovely but treated women either as a race apart or like men. I felt the feminine touch was needed. I really quite frightened the people at Plaistow, shocked them. I went to the vicar and asked him what exactly the church warden's duties involved. Then I went back to the middle-aged women (on the Parochial Church Council) who had said I couldn't have the job and asked them which of the duties of a church warden needed a penis. Of course, I blew my chances then, although I did eventually get the job because they couldn't get anybody else.

'It's the middle-aged women who tend to be the worst; the young ones are all right – and the old. The old ones take the attitude: "That's right, girl – have a go." '

One day in 1975 Ann gathered up her children and travelled to a bleak Essex aerodrome where a Diocesan Day was due to take place. It could have been a day more memorable for standing in endless queues for inadequate lavatory facilities than anything more spiritual, but it turned out quite differently: 'My salvation was in the loo queue. There was a lady queuing with a leaflet hanging over her arm. It was about women's ministry. I read it and it was like lightning striking. I knew it was what God wanted me to do. All my life fell into place – I mean, what better preparation could I have had – nursing and drama.' But the Church of England turned her down, recommending that she study for a degree in religious studies and perhaps try again at some later stage. Devastated, she nonetheless set about a correspondence course in religious studies and three and a half years later went back to another selection conference, a three-day affair, women only, and with the knowledge that only one in four would make it. This time they took her, and after a further twenty months of study she became a deaconess. It had taken five years from the day of the loo queue.

Being accepted by the Church gave Ann new confidence, and she admits that this was what led to the ending of her first marriage: 'I realised that I didn't have to go on being treated as rubbish.' Ann's subsequent experience demonstrates the inconsistency of the Church's position on divorce. As a divorcee, by 1987 she was eligible to be ordained deacon, but had she re-married, this would not have been possible. Yet she already planned to marry again prior to her ordination, but delayed her marriage until after she had become a deacon and it was too late for the Church to do anything about it. Her second husband, Christopher, is vicar of a neighbouring parish.

Since 1980 Ann Easter has been the parish worker in Stratford and chaplain to the maternity unit at Newham General Hospital. She has found her vocation – 'I've never stopped believing in God, only sometimes I've wondered whether He or She is good' – and for the foreseeable future her place, Stratford, because there is no career structure for ordained women in the Church of England and she has really got as far as she can go. Ann says parishes that have women have them as a 'liability', but in the same breath changes this to 'luxury'.

Her experience of running a parish, conducting funerals (for which she is much in demand, although one bereaved widow worried that it wouldn't be 'proper' with a woman, and when reassured asked whether it would be cheaper), religious broadcasting and Christian feminism, has proved both fulfilling and frustrating. She says that being able to preach in her Church – and since 1987 conduct weddings, baptisms and funerals – but not to be allowed to give Communion is like a couple being married all week and the man bringing in someone else to make love to his wife on Sundays.

Analogies aside, love, sex and the Church seem to her a healthy mix, and the 'lead us not into temptation' attitude adopted by the Bishop of London at the thought of a woman in charge at the altar ('My instinct when faced with her would be to take her in my arms . . . sexuality is built into human life and you cannot get rid of it.') meets with the response: 'I think he got it just right: it is a sexuality issue. But what does he imagine women have been thinking about dishy curates? Our sexuality is very much part of us, but perhaps the Church has spent so much time saying "thou shalt not", that people think they should leave their sexuality outside the church door and present their Sunday-best self – no smoking, no drinking, no lust. Quite the opposite of getting in the way, I think a person who is happy about their sexuality makes a much better priest – a more integrated and grown person all round.'

Dramatic statements are her style and she makes it plain that she felt cheated by the low-key staging of her ordination. After all the years of struggle she says it should have been in a cathedral, not the backwater parish church of Goodmayes, Essex, but having got so far she is more patient about the final step and is prepared to wait until 1992 rather than force the issue.

For Andrew and Lindsey Pearson 1992 will not be soon enough to avoid the pain and frustration of ordination for him and not for her. The Pearsons are both studying for the priesthood at Westcott House in Cambridge, where about a third of the students, and the staff, are women.

'Most women at Westcott feel they are being trained for the priesthood,' says Lindsey. 'But the Church will never admit that it might be selecting women as future priests,' adds Andrew.

The Pearsons met in Coventry in the early 1980s, where both were involved with community work backed by the Church of England. Lindsey has a social sciences degree and Andrew studied at agricultural college. Their decisions to seek ordination were made independently of each other, but they were married and both had been selected as candidates for ordination by the time they entered Westcott.

In 1989, they will together both be ordained to the diaconate, but in a year's time Andrew will become fully ordained to the priesthood and Lindsey will not.

'I think the difficulty will come then,' says Lindsey, 'when Andrew is ordained a priest and I am left sitting in the cathedral.'

Andrew too, feels the moment will be hard to cope with: 'I will have my own feelings of elation, but I think they will be greatly soured – having hands laid on me to allow me to take Communion services, while Lindsey, as a woman, can't have this. I feel it is unjust, but one has to be forgiving and tolerant and control oneself.'

Because they are married, the Pearsons don't want to work in the same parish when they leave Westcott: 'It would be too easy for us to be competitive – well, I would be,' says Lindsey. 'I think it is important that we are seen as having separate ministries.'

'If we were in the same parish, Lindsey would become the vicar's wife,' adds Andrew. 'The Church has not faced up to things. Lindsey has been selected to be trained as a deacon and I have been selected to be trained as a priest, but I didn't have to demonstrate more qualities than Lindsey.'

'I don't think there are that many differences between men and women,' she says. 'The differences are in the sort of people they are and in their background, but you have to try much harder as a woman, push much harder.'

Christina Rees is neither a 'religious', nor someone seeking ordination, but an active lay member of the Church of England, who regularly leads Sunday services in a small rural parish in Hertford-shire.

A life-long Anglican, she is American by birth and grew up at sea. Her parents had decided to travel the world in their own small yacht and educated their children themselves as the family sailed from port to port, High Church to Low Church.

'I went to a lot of churches of different denominations as a child, but it wasn't until I had grown up that I realised the differences do matter. Some people have a high view of the sacraments and some a low view. The high view would be scandalised to hear that I used to take Communion with friends sitting in a living-room. The Bible says, "When you meet together, do this in remembrance of me," and in 1970s California, where I was a student, I didn't know there could be anything controversial about "do-it-yourself" Eucharist. There are people who would get very upset about this and say it was not 'real', but it felt absolutely real at the time.

'I don't need that sort of thing now because I go to church regularly and I don't want to offend people, although what makes Communion different when a priest consecrates it, I don't know.'

Christina, who is in her early thirties, did her undergraduate work at Pomona in California, and then went on to study theology and broadcasting in Chicago. She says she obtained a deep sense of equality from reading the Bible, in particular – and perhaps surpris-ingly – from St Paul. ('There is neither Jew nor Greek, there is neither slave nor free, there is neither male nor female, for you are all one in Christ Jesus.' (Galatians 3:28)). She coped with the contradictions in Corinthians by studying hermeneutics, the science of interpretation of the Scriptures, translating what was written for mankind 2000 years ago to something individually relevant and meaningful for people today.

'For instance, I wear gold jewellery and I plait my hair and don't cover my head when I'm in church. Paul said all of this was wrong.'

She takes issue with those who argue in favour of strict adherence to the Bible: 'They are usually referring to the King James version, which, although it has the best flow and great beauty, is not the most authentic and probably the worst translation in terms of accuracy.'

Plaited, bejewelled and bareheaded, she leads the family service at her village church in Barley once a month, where attendance varies between thirty and sixty, there is plenty of congregation participation, and people say the atmosphere feels friendly.

'I plan the services but I speak without notes. I see myself as facilitating the worship. There is a couple who do not come to these services because they choose not to attend services that are led by women. I don't think I am being called to ordination, but I feel I do have a gift of leading and preaching.'

Christina is a member of her local Parochial Church Council, the Deanery Synod, the Diocesan Synod, the Bishop's Council, the Deanery Pastoral Committee and the Standing Committee of Deanery Synod. For three years she read and prayed and thought about women's ordination before 'coming out', as she puts it, at her deanery synod in St Albans: 'Some man had just been saying some really sad and hurtful things about why women couldn't be ordained. I stood up and said that the God I knew couldn't possibly care whether a priest was a man or a woman.

'I believe that the sexes are different and men do some things better than women, but priesthood is not one of them. Acoustically in church men are probably better than women; it will take a few years for women to gain confidence, and it's entirely a matter of conditioning. I know people who literally twitch when they hear a woman's voice in a church or cathedral because it doesn't sound right, but that's only because they are not used to it.

'Women are only just ready for priesthood. I meet a lot of intelligent women who are opposed to it. In my own experience, being young, female and lay, I am not legitimised. Recently, I organised a deanery Lent series over six weeks; we had guest speakers, prayers and singing, and many people expressed appreciation, but always implying that the ordained man, with whom I had shared the project, had done it all. People want women, and young women, to be involved in the Church, but they patronise us: it's always assumed that the man in the dog collar is the leader.'

Christina's view that women are only just ready for priesthood may or may not be true in the Church of England, but it was more than forty years ago that the first woman was ordained as a priest in the Anglican Church.

She was the Chinese Christian Florence Tim Oi Li, who, by all accounts, was neither militant nor ambitious. It was war that created the circumstances which led to her ordination and peace that forced her to renounce her priesthood.

Li Tim Oi was working as a deaconess in Macao in the 1940s. Before Hong Kong fell to Japan, a visiting priest would make the journey to Macao to celebrate the Eucharist in Li Tim Oi's parish, but travelling became so dangerous that it was suggested, as an exceptional measure, that she should be empowered to carry out the duties normally reserved to the priesthood. Her ordination took place in Xingxing after she had spent two years acting as a priest in Macao. The ceremony was conducted by the Bishop of Hong Kong, Ronald Hall, who was not an advocate of women's ordination. However, in January 1944 he wrote to the Archbishop of Canterbury reporting what he had done and proposing the regularisation of women priests in such circumstances. 'I have had an amazing feeling of quiet conviction about this – as if it was how God wanted it to happen rather than a formal regularisation first, which could result in women who "claim the right to be priests" pressing into ordination even where there was no real need of them as priests . . .' He went on to say that his action had nothing to do with any theoretical views as to the quality of men and women, but was simply an expedient in desperate circumstances.

The Bishop's letter ended with the words 'I do not expect you to approve', and he was right. The Archbishop accepted the idea of a woman being allowed to administer Holy Communion, but only as a deacon in situations where a man could not be there. He did not accept that Li Tim Oi could be ordained to the full priesthood, and at the first Lambeth Conference after the war this view was endorsed. Bishop Hall, who said he would not ask Li Tim Oi to resign her orders, was himself placed in the firing line. The situation was explained to Li Tim Oi and in 1946 she wrote to the Bishop, in effect, resigning. In her letter she described herself as a very tiny person, a mere worm, whose influence was very small compared with his. She said she did not have to keep the title of priest, that she did not need fame, but would continue her church work.

This she did, and has continued to do so ever since, but the issue of her ordination was only just beginning. In the journalist Ted Harrison's book *Much Beloved Daughter*, which recounts in detail Li Tim Oi's story, he says the Chinese bishops were in a quandary after the war. They could not afford to upset Lambeth because they needed financial help from Britain. The directive from Canterbury was unequivocal: Bishop Hall was to 'suspend the woman' because his ordaining her had been wrong. When it came to the vote by the Chinese House of Bishops, Li Tim Oi's resignation was accepted, although Bishop Hall abstained.

According to Ted Harrison, Li Tim Oi knew nothing of all the controversy surrounding her. She was busy resettling refugees in Macao while missives passed between Hong Kong and Lambeth Palace and before long she was to disappear for three decades into the Godless anonymity of Communist China. In more recent years, living in Canada, she has said she could see no theological argument against ordaining women and nothing to be gained by becoming a priest. It was simply a matter of the Church allowing men and women the same freedom to serve God. Her ordination had been ratified by the Chinese Church in Hong Kong in the 1950s (today, more than one third of theological students in mainland China are women) and in 1984 she came to Britain and was honoured in a special service in Westminster Abbey.

When the controversy over her ordination was at its height, she was sent to America for a holiday, but with strict instructions not to reveal herself as a priest. She did her best to obey but the word was out and the Americans wanted to hear her preach. On one occasion, in a group discussion, she was asked if she knew the famous woman priest in China causing such an upset in Britain. She did not reply. The holiday was cut short by events back in mainland China and she was summoned home.

For the Americans, who had been so keen to experience the ministry of a woman, a quarter of a century was to elapse before the ordination of women, but they have led the way in electing the first woman bishop. I was in America at the end of September 1988 when her election to the episcopate took place. Two or three days before this happened the general feeling was that it would not. The Rev. Linda Grenz at the Episcopal Church Office of Women in Mission and Ministry thought there was no chance, because voting was likely to be too split with four male candidates and two female. She felt sure the job would go to a man and that the whole election might have been arranged to achieve this (bishops in America are elected, unlike those in the Church of England, who are appointed).

In the event, the Rev. Grenz was to be proved wrong, and Barbara Harris, after eight ballots, defeated her nearest male rival by 276 to 224, to become suffragan bishop for eastern Massachusetts, the largest diocese in America, both in terms of geography and population.

'My phone was melting off the wall the night the news broke' the Rev. Janet Griffen, a priest in San Francisco, said a couple of days later. Ecstasy had travelled down the phone lines that night, but in the cold light of day Jan, as she is known by her parishioners, predicted a hard time ahead for the new bishop, who is fifty-eight, black and divorced. In a statement to the press, Barbara Harris said she would bring 'a sensitivity to the needs of different kinds of people, including minorities, women, the incarcerated, the poor and other marginalised groups'. Nevertheless, nine bishops of the Episcopal Church immediately declared themselves unable to be in communion with her, or accept any episcopal actions performed by her, specifically ordinations and confirmations. And in Britain, angry traditionalists demanded that the Episcopal Church withdraw from the Anglican Communion.

Of the 500 delegates involved in the election, several insisted that they were voting strictly on each candidates' merits, but press reports said it was clear in the nominating speeches that many participants were also thinking of history. And on 11 February 1989, more than 8,000 people witnessed the consecration of the first woman bishop at the John Hynes convention centre in Boston. Two people stood up and objected but they were boo'ed and jeered and left the ceremony, which included much clapping and the release of purple balloons.

There were no bishops from the Church of England present (except Hugh Montefiore who went as a member of the press), but the former UK moderator of the Movement for the Ordination of Women, Diana McClatchey, said she took with her greetings, congratulations and prayers from 100 individuals in the Church of England General Synod, including bishops, clergy and laity: 'We wanted to show Barbara Harris that some of us are fully in support of her, even though the Church of England cannot recognise her.'

In this country it was just on a hundred years ago that feminists began to make waves in the Church of England. They wanted some say in its government, and at a time when it was acting as a major centre of resistance to the women's movement generally. Anti-feminist doctrine came from the pulpit, and women who worked in the ministry were considered of the lowest order.

It was not until the 1920s that women parish workers began to approach professional status, although during the years of the Great War, with many of the clergy away on the battlefront, women had been allowed to lead the singing in church with the proviso that they could not dress up in surplice and cassock, or 'do' the leading from the chancel. Unlike the suffragettes, feminists in the Church did not cash in on this opportunity presented by war, nor really press the point when it was over. Even now, there are many people in favour of women's ordination who would find it completely unacceptable to employ the mildest of militant tactics, seeing banner-waving as bad form and inappropriate to the cause. The extent of 'militancy' in the 1920s was the appearance of one or two notable women in the pulpit at a time when women were not allowed to preach. These female forays into hallowed places brought outrage from the traditionalists, and the medieval notion that women were unclean because of menstruation, and therefore unfit for the ministry, was dredged up as reason enough to confine them to the pew.

The role and position of deaconesses in the Church of England seems to have caused some confusion over the years, and more than once campaigners for women's ordination have accused the Church of using the diaconate as a red herring. Few people outside the Church can be expected to understand that there is a difference between being a deaconess and a deacon (especially now that women can be either) and that women wearing dog collars seen marrying and burying people are ordained to the diaconate but not the priesthood. Even more confusing was the Church of Scotland's recent creation of a number of male deaconesses.

At the 1930 Lambeth Conference it was stated categorically that a deaconess was not a deacon, and that she could not assist at the sacraments. This did not change until very recently, and during the intervening years hardly a murmur was heard about ordaining women. The issue simply seems to have run out of steam until the 1970s, the great decade of feminism.

TWO

Equal opportunities and the Bible

For those who oppose the ordination of women there is no better starting point than the Garden of Eden. God made Adam first and then, to give him a bit of help, retrieved a rib and made Eve. It is too easy to dismiss this as fiction, to apply the same approach to all the Bible stories and look for the Will of God in worldly terms that make more sense; but if the bishops of the Church of England in their deliberations over women and the priesthood are still taking reference from the story of Adam and Eve then perhaps it should be taken seriously.

There are those on both sides of the debate over women priests who have found comfort and explanation in the story of the Creation. Those against have found the straightforward answer of 'man followed by woman', for ever in that order, but I heard an interesting interpretation from the Rev. Esmé Beswick of the Afro-Caribbean Pentecostal Church, who said the whole point was that woman came from Adam's side and that made her equal. Did this mean, I asked her, without wishing to be facetious, that if Eve had been created from Adam's big toe, she would have been deemed inferior? The answer was 'yes'.

Whether or not Eve started out equal, there is no doubt where she was by the time of Christ, disenfranchised and on a par with slaves, a position that was to change very little over the next two thousand years. There were exceptions in the Christian Church, women like the English St Hilda, a strong and of course chaste woman, Abbess of Whitby in the seventh century. Hilda was entrusted with the spiritual education of men who were to become bishops, but Hilda, like every woman in England before and since, was not deemed the right sex to be ordained herself.

If there can be a single reason why women have been kept out of the priesthood, then it must be either the war between the sexes or the will of God; and as this book has no pretensions towards theological scholarship, the latter has to be accepted as a possibility while the former is fair game for closer investigation. Theologians will claim that there are many different and complex scriptural interpretations involved in the issue, but it is, perhaps, disingenuous not to recognise sexism to be at the root of the whole debate.

In this, and coming chapters, there will be references to all manner of worship and divinity, including witchcraft and other 'slipstream' followings, but this book is principally concerned with what is happening in the Church of England and in mainstream Christianity, which is where the sex war has always been most evident. Christians, from the beginning, seem to have equated sex with the devil and feared it with equal terror and disgust; and because the social structure before and during Christianity's formative years gave dominance to men, it is hardly surprising that 'the weaker sex' got the blame for this tempting evil. Besides, hadn't Eve caused all the problems of the world in the first place?

Much of the misogynous thinking attributed to the early Christians seems to have come from St Paul, with his talk of man being the head of woman and her needing to maintain a low profile in order not to shame both man and God; although, as with the rest of the Bible, there can be found passages both for and against women, and quotations from Paul have often been misused in the sex war. Without going into detail at this stage it is perhaps most pertinent to the present point that he did say sex was 'no sin' (1 Corinthians 7:6–28). That he had to say this at all presupposes that the people to whom he was talking felt that it was. The inners of the female body were thought of by the early Christians as disgusting, and it seemed quite unacceptable that Jesus was born of a woman.

'To embrace a woman,' wrote Odo of Cluny in the twelfth century, 'is to embrace a sack of manure,' and the business of childbirth was considered to be so revolting that the Church Fathers wanted to remove Jesus as far as possible from the process – so much so that, even though Mary was known to have had other children after Jesus, she was to be designated 'Ever Virgin'.

The cult of Mary, 'Mother of God' has developed over the centuries, setting her apart from other women, so that even as late as the mid-nineteenth century Pope Pius IX made it an article of faith for all Catholics that Mary should be considered 'immaculately conceived' and from the moment of her conception incapable of sin.

Returning to the suggestion that early Christians must have viewed sex as a sin for Paul to have any reason to tell them that it was not, brings us to the enemy within – the driving force of sex within human beings that threatens to distract them from their God. Two thousand years on, good Christian men such as the Bishop of London, Dr Graham Leonard, are still worrying about this distraction, fearing that a woman at the altar will appear more like a sex object than a channel to God.

I say 'good' because it is, perhaps, this very 'goodness' that has given the male Christian his swollen conscience where women and sex are concerned. It could be argued that the more ancient civilisations had a less intense attitude towards 'the devil within'. In ancient Greece there was a practice known as sacred prostitution, intended to release for the common good the mysterious powers of fecundation. Herodotus reports that in the fifth century BC every Babylonian woman was expected once in her lifetime to give herself to a stranger in the temple of Mylitta for money, which she then donated to the temple.

Simone de Beauvoir, in her famous work, *The Second Sex*, explores these attitudes and practices and says that it is Christianity which invests woman anew with the frightening prestige she held in early history and that fear of the other sex is one of the forms assumed by the anguish of man's uneasy conscience. The Christian is divided within himself, she says, the separation of body and soul, of life and spirit, complete. Original sin makes the body the enemy of the soul, and all ties of the flesh seem evil. And, of course, since woman remains always the other, it is not held that both male and female are flesh: the flesh that is for the Christian the hostile 'other' is precisely woman. In her the Christian finds incarnated the temptations of the world, the flesh and the devil.

Simone de Beauvoir goes on to quote one of the first Fathers of the Church, Tertullian: 'Woman! You are the gateway to the devil. You persuaded him whom the devil dared not attack directly. Because of you the son of God had to die. You should always go dressed in mourning and in rags.' She then states that all Christian literature strives to enhance the disgust that man can feel for woman and, quoting Tertullian again: 'A woman is a temple built over a sewer.'

It is hardly surprising, with such pronouncements, that women were considered inferior beings and believed this themselves. For some while, they were not even credited with having souls; it was St Thomas Aquinas (1225–74) who decided that they had, dispelling a common belief at the time that women were descended from animals.

So, with the hypocrisy that has always dogged Christianity, man shifted the guilt within himself and blamed woman, with or without a soul, for his wretchedly distracting sexual urges and just about all the other 'evils' of the world stemming from the Fall. What is extraordinary is not this obsession with guilt and blame, but the fact that woman let him get away with it. Perhaps the most powerful argument for the belief that man is the superior being, and therefore the only one fit to be a priest, is the fact that after two thousand years of Christianity women are still fighting from behind. Women have still to reach parity, and even with the social handicap of childbearing and attendant limitations, it has taken an inordinate length of time for the female sex even to knock at the door of the Church and demand priestly status.

Women, both in the Old and New Testaments, are divided into just two categories: they are either wholly good or wholly evil – either in the Virgin Mary or the Jezebel mould. Presumably, by simplifying the problem of the 'other' in this way, it was easier for man to deal with the conflict within himself. Into the category of the good woman, who, like the Virgin Mary had little to do with sex, he could place his mother, wife and other female relatives. The rest could be lumped into the other category, begging the question again, why did women allow men to get away with it – allow themselves to be placed in one of two equally extreme, uncomfortable and unrealistic postures?

Of course, answers to such questions can always be found in the most basic facts of life, and it could be that women were too busy bearing children to have time to see or question where they were being placed. In Old Testament times polygamy was the rule rather than the exception, and the practice served a useful purpose in times and places where a nation was establishing itself, conditions of life were harsh, life-expectancy short, and the need for many children imperative. By New Testament times society was more established and it seems that in the first century of Christianity women were in quite a strong position, if only for a brief period.

Evidence of women in powerful and influential roles is well documented in Michael Walsh's *Roots of Christianity*, although he makes it clear that there was quite a gap between legal theory on the position of women in society, and actual practice. 'There is plenty of evidence from inscriptions of New Testament times that women made a major contribution to their cities. It is also clear that women went to court, transacted business and owned property quite independently of the husbands to whom they were supposedly subjected.' But there are conflicting reports of women's position in society at that time. The Babylonian Talmud has a story of the Galilean Rabbi Yose being scolded for merely asking a woman the way to Lydda: 'You stupid Galilean, have the sages not commanded "Do not engage in a lengthy conversation with a woman".' This is in line with first-century Jewish society, in which women were generally second-class citizens, banned from the inner courts of the temple, banned from any part of the temple during their monthly periods, and, at any time, instantly divorceable by their husbands. St Paul said they were to remain quiet at meetings since they had no permission to speak, and were to keep in the background because the Law dictated this; and if they had any questions, they should wait and ask their husbands when they got home.

Paul never knew the human Jesus and therefore he was reflecting the attitudes of contemporary society towards women rather than Jesus's own ideas, which appear to have been less repressive. With his Jewish ancestry Jesus would have known that in preceding centuries both men and women could speak out and claim to be representing the voice of God. These forebears were regarded as prophets, or *nabi'im* ('mouthpiece of God') and, although the Jews also had priests, a *nabi* was more important. In fact, the early Jewish priests had little status and their role was more to do with the practical details of religious ritual than with preaching and prophesying.

Women, usually the wealthy ones, were leaders in the early Church. Christians met in private houses and the gathering would be led by the head of the house, in many cases a widow. Baptism was a major door-opener for women: it replaced circumcision as initiation into the faith and could have been capitalised upon by women to a much greater degree; after all, baptism, as opposed to circumcision, took no account of the sex of the initiate and this might have been used as a strong indication of divine will towards equality.

The difficulty experienced by the early Christians was the same as Jesus would have had to contend with if he had chosen women to be his disciples. In the end it all boiled down to expediency. With the mood of the times it would have been even harder than it was anyway to establish a new religion if the social structures had been completely disregarded. Women did not have a public voice and therefore the message would not have been spread.

To this end, the power of women in the 'private' Church had to diminish, and by the end of the first century Christianity had capitulated to convention in order to gain the mass following it needed to survive.

Jesus's general attitude towards women seems somewhat ambivalent: perhaps they were only of interest if they were obvious sinners, prostitutes and the like – people, rather than just women, who needed to be 'saved'. Yet Michael Walsh writes that the first hints of Jesus's intention to spread the Christian mission outside Judaism came in two conversations he had with women – the Samaritan woman and the Syrophoenician woman – and the first witnesses to the resurrection were women.

Whether or not it can be argued that Jesus did more than most to treat women as equals, it is certain that they failed to hold on to any ground they had gained, and while there are plenty of quotable passages (from Paul, Timothy and others) on the subjugation of women, such as the following from Paul's first epistle to the Corinthians, there is nothing much in the way of feminist protest.

> What I want you to understand is that Christ is the head of every man, man is the head of woman, and God is the head of Christ. For a man to pray or prophesy with his head covered is a sign of disrespect to his head. For a woman, however, it is a sign of disrespect to her head if she prays or prophesies unveiled. She might as well have her hair shaved off. In fact, a woman who will not wear a veil ought to have her hair cut off. If a woman is ashamed to have her hair cut off or shaved, she ought to wear a veil.
>
> A man should certainly not cover his head since he is the image of God and reflects God's glory. For man did not come from woman; no, woman came from man; and man was not created for the sake of woman, but woman was created for the sake of man. That is the argument for women's covering their heads with a symbol of the authority over them, out of respect for the angels. However, though woman cannot do without man, neither can man do without woman, in the Lord; woman may come from man, but man is born of woman – both come from God. (11 : 3–12)

Despite all this, Paul allowed women to work with him as equals, and much of the content of his evangelism must have been extremely attractive to them, with its message of hope to the downtrodden. Yet, Christianity, like other religions, settled into an inevitable structure of inequality. Quoting Simone de Beauvoir again:

> There is a justification, a supreme compensation, which society is ever wont to bestow upon woman: that is, religion. There must be a religion for woman as there must be one for the common people,

and for exactly the same reasons. When a sex or a class is condemned to immanence, it is necessary to offer it the mirage of some form of transcendence. Man enjoys the great advantage of having a God endorse the codes he writes; and since man exercises a sovereign authority over woman, it is especially fortunate that this authority has been vested in him by the Supreme Being. For the Jews, Mohammedans, and Christians, among others, man is master by divine right; the fear of God, therefore, will repress any impulse towards revolt in the downtrodden female. One can bank on her credulity. Woman takes an attitude of respect and faith towards the masculine universe.

This seems to be one of the basic problems – that women have so often accepted and believed themselves to be inferior, clinging to the comfort of a message which amounts to 'You too can go to heaven.'

These thoughts and writings are concerned with the general character of woman over the centuries and the long acceptance of her secondary role to man; and the phraseology here gets at what is, perhaps, the nub of the problem for women who want to be priests: the passivity, the lack of sustained battle in the war between the sexes. The history of the priesthood as a Christian institution developed from the Jewish tradition, which was, of course, male and hereditary. The exclusive Christian sacrament, the Eucharist, now the single most important of all the sacraments and the 'big' one over which women have long been denied the right to preside, started out in first-century Palestine as an equal opportunities event.

The early 'priests', if we are to accept this term as applying to those empowered to mediate between God and mankind and to preside over the Eucharist, were either men or women, depending on who was the head of the house in which the service took place. It was only when things became more formal and systematised in the early centuries AD that women were cut out of the action – and allowed themselves to be, perhaps for the sake of unity, which is still a major issue. Undoubtedly, the involvement of women in the Eucharist would have caused division. Women playing such a central and visible role would have been unacceptable to the mainstream Jews who were not used to women even being present in their synagogues. Yet it was the opportunity for equality that attracted the hitherto underprivileged – women and slaves – to the new religion, making it all the more surprising that they allowed their chance to slip away so soon and without protest.

There were, as always, the 'breakaway' groups, among them some that continued to permit women leading roles: Marcionism, a second-century 'alternative' Church, was one. Marcion, who came from Asia Minor and settled in Rome in 144, maintained that Christianity was a completely new revelation quite unrelated to the Old Testament or the Jewish religion. He said there were two Gods, the Old Testament creator of the world, followed by the greater New Testament God of Jesus.

Church services devised by Marcion were almost exactly the same as orthodox ones, and there was a similar power structure of bishops, priests, deacons and deaconesses. Women were not allowed to be priests, but they could teach and prophesy, which did not accord with the orthodox dictum that women should keep quiet because they had no right to tell men what to do.

Montanism was another sect that offered women prominence, but here lies an interesting example of the Christian fear of sex and how it was tackled. Montanism, like Marcionism, eventually capitulated to the orthodox view where women were concerned, but Montanists had coped with the problem of women by being strictly celibate. Not much future in that.

It seems possible that the Christian fear of sex began as a reaction to the supposedly decadent times in which it all began, and was simply part of the Christian ideal of self-denial as shown by Christ's own example. Perhaps those early Christians, men and women, were sickened by the centuries-old pagan obsession with sex, the idolising of symbols that were overtly sexual. But, like so many a backlash against excess in one direction, they seem to have gone too far in another, creating a neurosis that still lies deep-rooted in twentieth-century Christianity.

Of course, the worst excesses of this reaction, which came to focus on women as the source of this and every other evil, were seen in sixteenth- and seventeenth-century Europe during the witch hunts. Christians, for centuries struggling with the guilt of their own sexuality and the belief that it was more of the devil than God-given, seized upon the notion of witches and their supposed association with Satan with a fervour just like the Nazis' persecution of the Jews, but lasting much longer. Christians in sexually neurotic Europe and, later, America at last had what they believed to be a God-sanctioned right to publicly torture and murder the witches, surrogates in their own desire to be rid of the devil and all his works. Again, this illustrates the old biblical division of women into just two categories, good and evil, and there were plenty of 'good' women anxious to emphasise this by pointing the finger at others.

All along, some women have played as big a part as men in persecuting and repressing their own sex, and even now there are as many (even more according to a recent MORI poll commissioned by *The Times*) women as there are men who don't want women to be priests.

The witchhunting handbook *Malleus Maleficarum* (*The Hammer of Witches*), produced in the fifteenth century by the Dominican Jacob Sprenger, made it clear that all witchcraft came from carnal lust, which in woman was already known to be insatiable, and to such a degree that she would consort even with Satan. It was therefore through women that the Devil could reach and gain power over mankind.

Sprenger explained women's evil by going back to the Creation and pointing out how there was a defect in the formation of Eve, as she was made from a bent rib. This meant that she was imperfect and would always deceive. It also made her weaker than man and more vulnerable to temptation.

In the *Malleus* (which was an early bestseller, going into nineteen editions) women, and not just witches, are roundly blamed, and Sprenger thanks God that men are free of sexuality and therefore witchcraft, 'for since He was willing to be born and to suffer for us, therefore He has granted to men this privilege'.

The writer Karen Armstrong comments in *The Gospel According to Women*:

The astonishing implication of this is that God did not save women or die for women, and therefore He has abandoned them to sex and thus to the Devil. There had always been a tendency to push women outside God's plan for the world; now they have been not only excluded but made to assume the position of an enemy, in alliance with the enemy of God and man.

It would seem, from this sort of thinking in the Middle Ages, that the only thing that could possibly save woman was man's desire for her. Such contortions of dogma and vain attempts by men to deny their own nature might seem outrageous and ridiculous, but are they so far removed from the present debate?

The Scandal of Particularity

Another starting point for the debate comes under this heading, which represents the thinking that it is scandalous to give God either gender, in which case why should the sex of a priest have any relevance?

The theologian and deacon Mary Hayter (a member of the Archbishops' Commission on Women and the Episcopate) points out that a growing number of feminists teach that the God/ess combines male and female characteristics, but that they, like those who assume that God is exclusively male, should remember that any attribution of sexuality to God is a reversion to paganism. But the Scandal of Particularity is a wider issue than that of God's gender. The scandal or 'disgrace' is that God should have taken human form, and at a particular time and in a particular place; and for some Christians it is almost beyond endurance that Christ's coming was so particular.

For many, if not all, of those against the ordination of women, the Incarnation made it clear that God chose to be represented as a male, but Mary Hayter says that the important thing was that Jesus came as a human being, not the fact that he was a man. It would not have made sense for him to have been born a woman at the time he came, but his sex should not affect the nature of the priesthood.

'The Scandal of Particularity is about a whole lot more than whether Jesus was born male or female. It seems limited and narrow that he was born into an ordinary family at all, that God, infinite, divine, should have chosen to pin Himself down to one little place and time in history.

'The roots of this are back in the Old Testament in His choosing the Jews, not to exclude other people but to use them as a channel. The Christian perspective is that the whole of God's work in human history with the Jews was working towards the birth of Christ, and part of the Scandal was that it was to be a once and for all "coming", that there would be no need for God to come again and again.'

This answered my question: why doesn't God manifest Himself again, now, as a woman, in order to even the balance? After all, in Genesis, He is reported to have created man and woman in his own image, which explains his adopting human, as opposed to, say, animal, form in the Incarnation, but not why He opted for maleness.

Mary Hayter has no problem with God the Father and God the Son. In fact she finds it offensive when Christ is depicted as female: 'This sort of thing focuses attention on the sexuality issue when it is not this that is important. Biological sexuality is not suggested by calling God "Father" and Jesus "the Son". Those against women priests say this is all-important, but this focusing on sexuality is the most unfortunate thing about the whole issue of women's ordination.' She feels that this leads to the upsetting and offensive suggestion from the 'anti' camp that all women who want ordination are undermining the heart of the Christian faith.

In his book *What Will Happen to God?* the Rev. William Oddie says that in the end, 'what is surely at stake in the whole feminist theological enterprise is whether or not we are prepared to receive God's revelation of Himself; whether, indeed there can be any such revelation'.

He goes on to quote C. S. Lewis:

> . . . Christians think that God Himself has taught us how to speak
> of Him. To say that it does not matter is to say that all the
> masculine imagery is not inspired, is merely human in origin, or
> else that, though inspired, it is quite arbitrary and unessential. And

this is surely intolerable: or, if tolerable, it is an argument not in favour of Christian priestesses but against Christianity.

Dr Oddie concludes:

Lewis was writing in the late nineteen-forties; forty years on, his words have a chilling and increasingly unmistakeable ring of prophetic truth. Whether, for the Anglican communion at least, the sound will be heard by generations to come as a warning note or as a funeral knell may depend on future events as yet only half guessed at.

In a later part of the book he refers to feminist theology, and the idea of God as Being – 'the power of being, the ground of being, rather than particular being'. 'The appeal of this kind of thinking to feminist theologians is clear enough,' he says, '. . . a way of talking about God which transcends "the alternative male-female", and which is capable of being developed against a one-sided male-determined symbolism.' Dr Oddie's own views are succinctly summed up in the final paragraph of his book: 'One thing seems certain: the more powerful the Christian feminist movement becomes, the more abundant will be the Church's bitter harvest of division, anger, suspicion and all uncharitableness.'

On the cover of Dr Oddie's book there is a somewhat misleading photograph of a feminist sculpture. It shows a female figure on the Cross – Christa crucified. This is the sort of imagery that offends the traditionalists and even those, like Mary Hayter, who represent radical re-thinking in theology yet cling to scriptural detail, despite the scandal of its particularity.

Tackling the Christa idea head on, there are Christians who argue that Christ had to be a man because if he had been Christa, man would have been entirely superfluous as a servant to God. The accolade of personal service to Christ was given first to Mary, his mother, and then to the group of women who surrounded him to supply his earthly needs.

Elaine Bishop, a prominent member of WAOW, Women Against the Ordination of Women, has said: 'Unless she [Christa] had been born of a male virgin, the male sex would have been completely excluded from the work of redemption, so Christ chose men as his apostles and through them gave the sacramental priesthood to the male sex: "Here is a little corner where they, too, may serve the Lord directly, at his altar. For this office no gifts of mind or body are required." '

The thinking behind this is that women are already more favoured in the eyes of God, and that His assignment of the priesthood to men was merely a concession to stop them feeling left out. It's a neat, but rather tortured piece of reasoning. There seems to be within it a disingenuous downgrading of the priesthood that must equally offend both men and women who feel called to that office.

Mary Hayter attributes the predominance, in both Old and New Testaments, of masculine imagery as representative of God's power and authority to the culture of those times. She says the very 'particularity' of the scriptural documents demands that we acknow-ledge the economic, social and political differences between those circumstances and our own, and then that we read the texts with critical respect in order to distinguish the timeless truths of Scripture from its more culturally conditioned aspects. Dr Hayter, who sees herself as an orthodox Christian believer, feels that this is the only way of re-establishing the authority of the Bible for today; that critical study of Scripture is not 'an optional extra' to faith, but essential to true understanding, which, in her view, includes equality for women in modern doctrine.

Tinkering with tradition
and the emasculation of the Church

Re-defining Scripture in this way, tinkering with tradition and the interpretation of particularity, is of course unacceptable to many orthodox believers. Dr Oddie, who describes himself as an 'ordinary, *Daily Telegraph*-reading Anglican', said at a recent Cambridge Union debate: 'No one seems to know any more what Anglicans are supposed to believe. We must all now make it up as we go along.' The motion being proposed was: 'This house has no confidence in the present leadership of the Church of England.' Dr Oddie spoke in favour of the motion, opening his speech with the words: 'The Church, in its history, has never been adequate to its task.' He also referred to the controversial Preface to Crockford's 1987–8 *Clerical Directory* written by Gareth Bennett (who later committed suicide after threat of disclosure), describing it as the 'manifesto of the silent majority', and adding: 'There's been a dreadful emasculation of the Church.'

The Bennett Preface, which says a lot of unkind things about the Church of England, the Archbishop of Canterbury and the issue of women's ordination, amounts to a detailed description of this emasculation – if emasculation it is. Gareth Bennett was obviously very much against the ordination of women, seeing it as divisive and symptomatic of a Church compromising its sacred traditions.

Those in agreement with this doubtless also concur with Dr Bennett's final paragraph, headed 'Black people in the Church', in which he called for the elimination of 'any kind of discrimination' – an appeal that must have been noted by the women and men, black and white, who are asking for sexual equality in ministry.

Returning to the Cambridge Union debate which resulted in a massive defeat for the traditionalists, the final speaker and opposer of the motion, Bishop Hugh Montefiore, particularly suited to the priesthood not only because of his maleness but also because of his Jewish birth, declared himself in favour of women priests and said he had actually ordained one in America.

It was unfortunate that he, like just about everyone else, referred to the quite separate issues of homosexual clergy and women's ordination in the same breath, but his conclusion on the women issue was 'get the agony over quickly'. In other words, the Church should ordain women to full priesthood sooner rather than later.

That the question of women's ordination was central to the debate is hardly surprising, any more than its being lumped together with other areas of deviance from traditional received understanding of Scripture. Mary Hayter feels that women's ordination is being used as a 'scapegoat' by the traditionalists, who see it as part of other, what she would say were unrelated, issues such as changes to the Prayer Book, morality and what is believed doctrinally.

'It is not that the Bible provides the "last word" for or against women's ministry,' she says. 'Such finality is unlikely, since biblical writers were not concerned with the question in the form in which it must be considered by modern ecclesiastics and scholars. Rather, as C. H. Dodd put it in *The Authority of the Bible*, "if the Bible is indeed 'the Word of God', it is so not as the 'last word' on all religious questions, but as the 'seminal word' out of which fresh apprehension of truth springs in the mind of man".'

Whether this sort of interpretation constitutes use or abuse of the Bible in the debate about women depends, of course, on whether you are for or against women priests. But to an outsider, with no theological axe to grind either way, detailed study and interpretation of Scripture seems more likely to produce a recipe for confusion than revelation of truth. It is, perhaps, as scandalously particular as the Scandal of Particularity.

It is true that the law at the time of Christ would have made it very difficult for women to enjoy prominence, to be leaders, to have a public voice; and that to survive, the early Church needed to settle into social convention. However, the argument is lost when compared with the law as it stands today in Britain: the Church of England, the established Christian Church, has for some years gone against civil law in not allowing women equal opportunities. Those in favour of women priests might argue that, just as the early Church needed to conform to survive, the same applies today and that women priests could be the single most powerful means of bringing people back to the Church. Equally, those against ordaining women will argue that to allow women's ordination would divide the Church and bring about its demise. History does not give us the answer. All it does is chronicle guilt and repression and the ongoing war between the sexes, throughout which, one could say, miraculously, Christianity has so far survived.

THREE

The male preserve

Dr Johnson once said that a woman preaching was like 'a dog's walking on his hinder legs. It is not done well; but you are surprised to find it done at all.'

Two centuries on, in December 1988, it was disclosed in the *Sunday Times* that nearly 3,000 clergymen, among them 20 bishops and 11 archdeacons, still believed the priesthood to be the male preserve. Stories of clergymen who take this view simply because they don't think women would be up to the job, are inferior to men, or sound too shrill in church, seem to be verging on the apocryphal. The silly sexism of the kind Dr Johnson got away with is heard more from the laity, people like journalist Richard Ingrams, who is equally mischievous and unkind in what he writes. In his column in the *Observer* he has more than once expressed his prejudice. In May 1988 he wrote:

> Last Sunday in Washington I had my first experience of a woman priest . . . Perhaps it was the combination of a woman and an American accent which prevented me from feeling in a very religious mood. Whatever the reason, I left [the cathedral] with all my prejudices confirmed. In place of a sermon we were given a dualogue between a senior Episcopalian cleric and a feminist Roman Catholic nun. It was during this, when the cleric was droning on about the great revolution taking place in the relationship between the sexes, that I got a sense of how much boredom we are in for if ever the woman-priest idea gets off the ground.

The previous month, in the same newspaper, he wrote:

The first thing I heard on Thursday morning was a woman with a droopy voice on Radio 4's *Prayer For Today*, thanking God for the 'feminine, motherly side of Christ'. (This act of thanksgiving was inspired by the Gospel story when, after his resurrection, the disciples find Jesus cooking fish on the seashore. Just like a mum, you see.) . . . Another deaconess, appearing on *Panorama*, was heard to say that the only difference between her and the vicar was that the vicar had a penis. Even as an anatomical statement this strikes me, if one is going to talk in those terms, as pure balls . . .

I have always felt the strongest possible aversion to the whole idea of women priests. Not being a theologian, however, I have found it necessary to justify my feelings logically. I was coming round to the idea that perhaps, after all, it was just a good old-fashioned case of what we journalists call prejudice. But I am now beginning to think that there is one very sound reason for not having women as priests – that they wouldn't be any good at it.

This sort of prejudice is by no means solely the male preserve. Take the parish matron on the April 1988 BBC *Panorama* programme: 'A woman vicar – no thank you!' A comment like this is said by the pro-women priests lobby to represent a fixation with the idea that priests have to be men, and as such, many feel, deserves the deepest compassion. The trouble is that there will, for a long time, be plenty of fuel for this attitude, particularly from America. 'American priest gives birth to "sperm gift" baby', as reported in the *Daily Telegraph* in December 1987, must have been seized upon with glee by the 'anti' brigade in the conservative pasturelands of traditional Anglicanism. The unfortunate Rev. Lesley Northup, a forty-year-old New York spinster described as intense and articulate, proclaimed that she had done nothing illegal or immoral when inseminating herself on three successive nights in December 1985 with sperm from three different, carefully chosen donors. Two of them were priests, but as both were single and their masturbation intended for procreation the whole exercise had received the blessing of Church leaders.

It is hardly surprising that a few days after carrying this story, *Telegraph* readers were regaled with 'Pregnant "priests" are not wanted here' in a letter from the Rev. Anthony D. Couchman, London E17: '. . . The Rev. Lesley Northup feels that she has done nothing to violate her vows to live her life as a "wholesome" example of Christian precepts. She may not; but I imagine that most Christians were quite sickened by the disgusting episode.'

Reaction of this kind seems to have much of traditional Christian disgust and guilt over anything sexual. Indeed, priests are supposed to be sexless, as evidenced by the dreary, colourless clothes they wear by tradition, dressing up only when in church to give glory to God. This supposed sexlessness rather contradicts the argument that priests can be of one sex but not the other, yet in the 1966 Report of the Archbishops' Commission on Women and Holy Orders it is stated: 'The view that sex is irrelevant is no longer tenable. There is in fact a masculine and a feminine human nature with some complication from the shadow of the opposite sex in each.'

The same report under the heading 'Why the Christian Priesthood is Male' says: 'It is quite legitimate to say that the exclusion of women from Holy Orders is just part of the nature of things, in this case of the nature of the Christian Church.'

This 'nature of things' argument is vividly expounded in the report in a paper entitled 'Women Priests' by the Rev. S. R. P. Spilsbury:

> The true celebrant of the Eucharist is Christ, the spouse of the Church; but since we are now in the realm of the Sacraments, Christ presides in and through the minister – the bishop or the priest – who represents him. However, the minister must be a naturally apt symbol of Christ, just as all the sacramental symbols must be naturally apt for their function. One could not baptise with ink, for how could that signify cleansing? One could not use poison in the Eucharist, for how could this signify Christ's nourishment of the faithful? One could not have a true marriage between two people of the same sex, and so on. By the same token, I suggest, a female priest could not be, from the very nature of the case, an apt symbol of Christ as presiding over his people in the Eucharistic meal, since Christ as Head of the Church stands in a relation which is symbolised by the relation of male to female. Because of this, a woman is not an appropriate subject to receive the order of priesthood.

As Brian Heeney says in his book *The Women's Movement in the Church of England 1850–1930*, published posthumously in 1988, advanced Church feminists first raised the matter of ordination to the priesthood in the press a few years before the First World War, denouncing the alleged self-interest of male priests in monopolising their profession. This was in April 1910 and brought shocked and spirited opposition. 'The universal custom of the church from the first, not to mention a sense of decency and propriety, apparently goes for nothing,' wrote one clergyman, 'but surely a joke is intended,' he added hopefully. Another referred to the idea as a 'wicked return to the ideals of heathenism', which would drive men away from both the ministry and congregations.

Brian Heeney continues: 'A scriptural argument was produced which was to be used by opponents of women's ordination to the priesthood for over sixty years to come: that Jesus had chosen men as apostles, and in so doing defined the ordained ministry as a male preserve for all time.'

The unnamed 1910 opponent linked women priests with heathenism, yet ancient cults have been used as further evidence for justifying the male preserve and are referred to in official Church of England reports such as *Women and Holy Orders* (1966). Under a section headed 'Why the Christian Priesthood is Male', V. A. Demant explains that it is all to do with 'deep hidden roots' that Christianity shares with most other religions, including Brahmanism, Buddhism, Islam, Judaism and the Olympian Greek cults.

Demant points out that, although in most fundamental respects Christianity represents a revolutionary force in the religions of the ancient world, the Christian Church, without question, scruple or argument, adopted a male priesthood. To change this and allow female priests might tamper with the foundations of belief and the psychic effects of the faith. He says that the force of any religion is in the living impact of a concrete religious culture. This culture consists of beliefs, rituals, organisations and an area of faith which is below the level of conscious belief. The maleness of the official ministry is a manifestation of the whole package, and to isolate it and claim that it is accidental and replaceable is to run the risk of undermining the whole religion.

> Therefore to have a twin priesthood of males and females could be
> more disruptive of the Christian Church than any doctrinal heresy
> or moral deviation. That is because we are here dealing not only
> with the conscious, intellectual and ethical side of Christianity but
> with the deep hidden roots from which religions and their
> distinctions spring.

Six years later, in a further report entitled *The Ordination of Women to the Priesthood*, Prebendary Henry Cooper, while accepting equality between the sexes, talks of natural theology and the order of creation, making it clear that a proper initiative rests with the male: 'even if it often has to be elicited by the female'. He continues:

> Although normally the woman is paramount as the centre of the
> family, the man is normally the link between the family and society
> at large. For these reasons a good Creator has endowed each with
> the appropriate qualities, for families need a strong skilful person to
> fend for them and defend them, whilst they need a tender protective
> person to cherish them. This is not to say that in necessity the
> sexes cannot, with difficulty, reverse their roles, but do we want
> *ab* normal women in the ministry?

More forcefully, the report goes on to say that women who try to do men's jobs are seen as betraying their sex and abandoning their calling, reducing them to mere substitute men, unaware of their own different and parallel dignity: 'a dignity particularly revealed by those women saints who demonstrate a continuous and unfailing acceptance of humble dependence on God'. This is followed by a description of how some women see themselves as made to work for men, always to be second in command, to help and advise rather than to govern, because they feel physically and psychologically inferior, if not spiritually and intellectually. The report asks: 'What are the consequences of these understandings of the man–woman relationship for the ordination of women?'

The conclusion is that the nature of priesthood has to be connected with a natural law that subordinates women, making it

appropriate to entrust the conduct of formal public acts of the
Church's worship to the dominant sex. Furthermore, the report
states that sex occupies a more central place in feminine human
nature than in the masculine, and therefore the appearance of
women as leaders of worship and ministrants of the sacraments
would destroy the sexless and impartial tone which 'at present'
marks Christian worship.

I have put 'at present' in quotes because this report came out in
the early seventies and, although it still holds good for a substantial
minority of the Church of England, there has been a huge shift of
opinion. It is now commonplace to have experienced the leadership
of women in worship (if not in ministering the sacraments) and the
idea that this destroys the sexless and impartial tone is largely seen
as specious. This is not to say that prejudice against women clergy
is disappearing, only that its more obvious expressions are no
longer intellectually tenable. This has been enforced by the appointment of women in some of the historical bastions of the male
preserve, even if the old guard is still up.

When the Chaplain of Clare College, Cambridge first walked into
the common room her instinct and her training made her want to
get everyone talking and engaged in interesting conversation; but
the all-male assembly were silent behind their newspapers and that
was how they wanted to remain.

Vivienne Faull, the first woman chaplain to an Oxbridge college,
tells the story with good humour and more against herself than her
silent colleagues, who have since come to see her as 'Viv', as
opposed to a woman in a man's job. So how much prejudice has she
encountered since her arrival at Clare in the mid-eighties, her
subsequent ordination to the diaconate, and election to the General
Synod's House of Clergy?

'There's been no backlash from the students,' she says. 'It's a bit
like kids thinking that prime ministers are women, they've never
known anything different; but, yes, from the clergy there has been
reaction.'

Vivienne believes there are some clergy who became so because it was a profession which excluded women. These, she says, are the traditionalists, the men who feel threatened by women, fearful that they might do the job better. There are also those who feel the job will be downgraded if women are allowed full ordination, and those who feel compelled to undermine the women who are nearly there. At a recent Synod, Vivienne was greeted by a fellow representative in the House of Clergy. He recognised her as a deacon by the colour of her Synod badge (pink for the House of Clergy) and remarked on the absence of her dog collar, quickly adding that he did not allow the woman deacon in his parish to wear one either. It was unbecoming on a woman, he opined, besides which, the woman in question had no dress sense anyway and was generally 'scatty'.

'Are you scatty too?' he continued.

'Probably,' Vivienne replied, hackles risen; although not completely, she added, or she would not have been able to do her job at Clare.

'His attitude changed completely when he found out where I worked. He then started to ask me difficult theological questions. It was interesting – his need to control.'

Of the General Synod's three voting Houses (Bishops, Clergy and Laity), all of which have only minorities against women priests, but sufficient to prevent the overall two-thirds majority needed for change, it is in the House of Clergy that the main opposition resides. The reasons for this opposition range from the theological through to the blatantly sexist, although it could be argued, superficially, that there is not much difference between these two extremes, that the theological objections are simply sexism cloaked in scholarly terms. Somewhere between the two lies the case for unity, the view that no issue can be more important than unifying the Christian Church, and until this is achieved the question of women's ordination should be put aside.

This is the view of the Rev. John Mullett, Rector of Ashwell in Hertfordshire, a man who throughout his long ministry in this country and abroad has worked alongside deaconesses and women lay-workers, and whose elder sister, a Whitby nun, has spent a lifetime at the sharp end of ministry, teaching and leading com-

munities in Africa. One of her triumphs was the creation of a school
for African women after she had complained to her bishop that
everything was being done for young African men, and nothing for
the women. But Sister Stella Mary does not want women priests,
and later in this chapter she will be explaining why.

My introduction to her brother came via his son. John (junior) is
in favour of women's ordination and had told me about discussions
with his father, who has always been against. It is interesting that
when I told John about the book and that I needed to talk to
clergymen 'against', he said: 'My father will speak to you. He's
retiring soon, so he's not going to be worried about his bishop's
disapproval or anything like that.'

This comment said a lot more about current sentiment in the
Church of England than it did about the Rev. Mullett's personal
circumstances. The possibility that there could be 'closet' clergymen
up and down the country, keeping quiet their opposition to women's
ordination for fear of losing preferment, is almost unbelievable. To a
lay person, there is an image of priestly vocation which would seem
to put them above such considerations of ambition, but it is this
very image, conditioned by the notion of priesthood as a superior
state of being, that is challenged by many of those in favour of
women's ordination.

Some of the stories of innate male arrogance in Christianity, as in
other areas of life, are amusing, even rather endearing. I particularly
liked one I found in the 1972 report presented by the Advisory
Council for the Church's Ministry under the title *The Ordination of
Women to the Priesthood*. Within the section headed 'Tradition' is
recorded the story that when Bernard of Clairvaux was kneeling
before a statue of the Virgin, she opened her lips to speak, but he
said, 'Silence, it is not permitted to a woman to speak in the church.'

John Mullett (senior) let me borrow this report and others on the
subject of women's ordination, pointing out that it might be interesting to see which passages he had underlined. I did this, and the
common thread seemed to be a placatory approach towards women
in the Church: let them do everything bar the Eucharistic ultimate —
the male preserve. His reason for opposing women's ordination to

the priesthood is quite straightforward: unity with Rome and the Orthodox Churches is, to him, the great issue and one about which he has been passionate all his ordained life. As a young priest he believed that this unity was imminently achievable. As a priest nearing retirement, he sees it as a long way off and attributes this reversal entirely to the issue of women priests. It is a great sadness and disappointment to him, especially as, in his own experience of serving congregations in Africa and India, in the industrial North of England, inner London and in the country parish of Ashwell, he says he has never felt that there has been any strong desire for the ordination of women. And yet he says: 'For sixteen years, before I came to Ashwell, I always worked alongside a full-time woman minister, deaconess and Church Army sister. I'll guess I've listened to more sermons from a feminine voice than any Bishop of the Bench. Every lively parish deserves a good deaconess.'

So why not a woman priest? The Rev. Mullett, although citing unity as his principal reason for opposing women's ordination, is also a traditionalist, but a humble one. He talked of symbolism and Christ's masculinity, and then went on to say that the secular world mistakenly thinks of a vicar as being the 'managing director' and head of the local church, whereas his calling is, in fact, to 'serve' the church's congregation: 'In no way is his calling superior. The sexes, I believe, have complementary, but equal gifts. There is none greater than to be a Christian mother or teacher, doctor or nun.'

All this accords with his 'underlinings' mentioned above, and his opposition to the idea of 'rank' in the Church; but it can hardly be denied that there is a ranking system in the priesthood, and this led me to ask him about the plight of younger priests who share his views. Could it really be possible that they kept quiet about their opposition to women's ordination for fear of damaging their career prospects?

'I have no direct evidence of anybody who, if asked, would tell an untruth, but I do believe that a lot of people would keep a very low profile on the matter and be careful of what they say. I feel sorry for these younger men. I can speak freely because I am near the end of my active ministry. The whole issue has been badly handled by the Church of England. Men and women have been so hurt.' It was hard to believe that here was the man who insisted that a visiting Ugandan missionary, the Rev. Deborah Micungwe, remove her clerical collar before entering his church, a story which has become legend in the diocese. As I left him and his Georgian rectory, its garden abundant with cow parsley, he agreed that the women priests issue was indeed momentous, but argued that it really had nothing to do with the equality of the sexes.

During my visit to John Mullett he suggested that I should talk to his colleague in the nearby parish of Weston: 'He's against, but he'll give you a very different view from mine.'

The Rev. Martin Dudley is a much younger man, brought up a 'high' Baptist (if there can be such a thing), who converted to Anglicanism when he realised that this was, in practice, what he had been all along.

I suppose I had gone along to the vicarage at Weston hoping, with journalistic avarice, that I was about to interview a male chauvinist pig in a clerical collar, a priest who would come out with the sort of stuff that makes Christian feminists spit teeth. Instead, I discovered that his position had changed.

Until about a year ago, the Rev. Dudley, a theologian, was outspokenly against women priests on theological and personal grounds. The personal are the more interesting. Asked, before his 'conversion' whether and why he felt threatened by the possibility of women being ordained, he answered that, yes, he did, but it wasn't the masculine in him that felt this threat, it was the feminine.

'We are not men's men,' he would say. 'We listen and we are receptive to people, that is what a priest has to be. Who is going to want us for this work if there are women priests who may do it better?'

Alongside this personal sense of threat, Martin Dudley used to feel that the authority of theology was on his side, and therefore he could comfortably go on voting against women's ordination at his diocesan synod. That was until he began a re-assessment of the theology upon which much of the 'anti' argument is based. Romish by inclination, he had already accepted the Vatican's rejection of

any medieval doctrine that viewed women as inferior, and many of
the old Bible-based arguments he had dismissed as incomprehensible.
He then found himself unconvinced by biblical material such as the
matter of male 'headship' propounded by Paul: 'Scripture doesn't
help. I'm not deeply impressed by biblical arguments.'

This questioning (he believes that theology will always be an
open-ended question) and re-assessment coincided with his meeting a
group of Catholic nuns seeking ordination, and an American woman
studying at Cuddesdon prior to her ordination. He feels that these
meetings were providential. 'Ordination is about power to consecrate the Eucharist and there is no reason why a woman can't do
this, why a woman can't be a priest.'

This much said, he adds that there is still a second question,
which is, *should* a woman be a priest?

'One should not discard tradition too easily; it is not a dead hand.
We have to be very careful about tampering with it. We have to
consider authority and how it works in Anglicanism. When the
General Synod said there was no fundamental objection to the
ordination of women this was clearly rubbish, otherwise why didn't
they go ahead there and then? There are fundamental objections by
some members. We should have all done it together. The Americans
went ahead without thinking it through. There are many who
believe that the greatest thing the Spirit guides us to now is unity,
but you can't have your cake and eat it and, at the moment,
ordaining women to the episcopate will prejudice unity.

'I am keeping my head down and not saying anything. I am not
making a secret of my changed mind, but the issue is too damaging
to the unity of the Church.'

This, of course, disregards unity with women in the Church who
want to be ordained, but perhaps they don't amount to a large
enough slice of the unity 'cake'. Martin Dudley thinks that it could be
the next century before an Anglican woman is fully ordained in
England. He feels that the next General Synod could be more
conservative in composition and throw out the proposition, putting
it back at least another five years. So is this the reason why he is less
concerned, less threatened, because the evil day is likely to be put off?

'I would not leave the Church if women were ordained,' he said, as if answering from his earlier conviction. 'I don't think one should encourage things that cause major disunity. For the moment it seems fair to say I'm not opposed, but neither am I a proponent. I don't want to see a victorious MOW – I don't like them. We can't think that having women ordained will solve the problems of women in the Church. I find it very sad that the flower rota, the coffee rota – all those sorts of jobs – are all done by women in my parish. There ought to be more men doing these things.'

Flower rotas aside, what will happen if women are kept out by the next Synod? Martin Dudley is concerned that the activists will run out of patience and take illegal action, bringing ordained women from overseas to preside over the Eucharist, not, as hitherto in halls and private homes but in churches; that rebel bishops will go ahead and ordain and in so doing violate the laws of the realm. 'The consequences could be very serious. We could see bishops being sent to prison.'

'A lot of women I know could make better priests than the men who are,' Sister Stella Mary told me a few weeks later. 'But this doesn't mean they should be ordained.' I met her a day or two after her return to England from Johannesburg, where she has spent the past few years leading a retreat house. An Anglican nun with the Order of the Holy Paraclete at Whitby in Yorkshire, Sister Stella Mary resisted her vocation for some time, thinking God had made a mistake. A science graduate, she had gone out to Africa to teach, and encouraged her parents and brother to join her: 'Everyone was out there but I felt I had to come back to England. I had been building a school – literally – and was very happy getting it launched, but I had this feeling that God didn't want my work, He wanted me; there is quite a difference between what I am and what I do. I put it off for two years but eventually I made up my mind to go.'

The place she went to was a castle, the Whitby home of her Order, founded during the First World War. She believed she had been called to this specific Order and the 'test' of her vocation proved positive, although within a short time she was back in

Africa, in the rain forests of Ghana, teaching 'A' level chemistry in the jungle. Some years later she returned to England and was appointed to the chaplaincy at Nottingham University, the first woman in the post.

'We take a vow of obedience, which means I am quite free to go where God wants me. Officially I am a lay person in the Church, but I feel absolutely fulfilled. At Nottingham I did everything except preside at the sacraments. It is socially recognised that some jobs are interchangeable between men and women but the priesthood is quite different. I never have seen it as a job; it has nothing to do with the treatment of women in secular life. It is quite separate. The whole of humanity is in God, but the male priesthood is part of a revealed truth which does not have to be explained. It is part of the mystery of God and I am not happy about human beings tampering with these things.'

Sister Stella Mary says that many people ask her what she 'does' as a nun, but it is what she 'is' that means more. Vocation, she says, is a calling to *be* something, not to *do* something: 'We are not just do-gooders. Being a sister comes first and it is the same with priests; it is what they are that is most important, rather than their suitability for the job.' She believes the campaign for the ordination of women is to do with human desire for betterment, an inadequate reason, and one to be regarded with suspicion.

This kind of thinking is easily shot down if one is limited by secular comparison, but that there may be virtue and truth in it is at the heart of the whole issue.

On a more superficial level, it would seem that this is where a look at the clerical collar might be appropriate. There is no other symbol that so immediately marks out a priest and, some would say, nothing that looks more ridiculous around the neck of a woman. Indeed, there are women in MOW who, if ordained, would not want to wear the collar, who see it as representing a priesthood they want to change. They don't want to be seen as substitutes for men, and neither do they want to perpetuate a hierarchical priesthood, one that seems to elevate the ordained above the laity.

There is plenty of conflicting opinion about the collar, but how did it originate, this small and unnecessary item of dress, that is more masculine than trousers? A lot of people I asked, chiefly vicars, didn't know. It was the Rector of Ashwell who suggested that I contact Watts, the vestment makers in Westminster, who explained that the present-day clerical collar is more correctly the Roman collar, which began to be worn in Rome during the nineteenth century. Collars before then were brocade bands of linen and not so distinguishable from those worn by other professional men such as barristers, but the true origin of today's 'dog' collar is more academic than clerical. Watts describe it as based on a development from academic dress, as seen even now during degree ceremonies at Oxford and Cambridge. More revealing (and, perhaps, ironical), Watts say the Roman collar is also connected with the opening up and re-awakening of the Church of England in the last century following its eighteenth-century hibernation. The old insularity was to be breached, and clerical fashion influenced by European trends.

Whatever the origin, the collar today can be both an inhibitor and a door-opener, depending, probably, on who is wearing it. Vivienne Faull, Chaplain at Clare College, Cambridge, said she found it difficult to get into hospitals outside visiting time without a collar. Baptist minister Ruth Matthews, agreed, but said she would still not wear it: 'I could never face having those masculine things – it literally means dressing up like a man. Women with them on are odd-looking. People are more relaxed if they don't see a collar.'

Cathy Milford, who ran a parish in Bradford for two years, said her parishioners loved it when she was ordained deacon and started to wear a collar: 'They approved. They said it looked good on me and made it clear who I was. It is a very clear statement, although I have experienced opposition and that turns your stomach over, people calling me sarcastically "Your reverence" and "Your eminence".'

East London deacon Ann Easter says she likes wearing a clerical collar because it makes it clear to everyone who she is: 'I reckon I can get in anywhere with it. I always wear full clerical dress.' But she has a couple of dog collar stories to tell:

'I was talking to a modern, educated woman in her mid-thirties and she told me she was quite shocked to see me in my collar. She said she felt I had gone over to the other side, that I had left her.

'On another occasion, soon after I was ordained, I was driving back from a funeral when I saw a colleague's wife who is a nursing sister. I had been using some pessaries for pre-menstrual tension and having some difficulties, so I stopped and went across the road and started telling her about my problem. She said she never thought she would have such a conversation with someone wearing a clerical collar.'

Patricia Pinkerton, ordained in the United States, feels that women need to wear the collar to show their equality with men, at least until women are established in the Church: 'There are women who wear converted lace blouses and the clergy collar underneath. I wear a black shirt or blouse. Pinks and frills make women look like second-class citizens. Until women are ordained it is important to have that professional look. We don't want to have the "pulling out the powder puff" look.'

Whatever the benefits, or otherwise, of wearing a collar back to front, the comment I like best came from Roman Catholic activist Alexina Murphy, who said it was just as well tonsures had gone out.

FOUR

Nearly but not quite – parishes run by women

The Church allows and expects women who are active in ministry to do all the 'donkey work' and more, but their position in the parish is rather like that of an able and conscientious secretary who finds herself running the business in the absence of the boss. She has all the knowledge and ability for the job, but authority, title and recognition are never officially conferred.

As deaconesses, women, their training equal to their ordained male colleagues, could provide all the pastoral support and preparation for the sacraments of baptism and marriage, but were prohibited until 1987 from actually performing the ritual of the event. The change in 1987, which enabled women to enter the ranks of the ordained and progress from deaconess to deacon, was a major breakthrough, allowing them to perform nearly all the Holy Sacraments but still barring them from presiding over the most frequent and most important, Holy Communion. So women who run parishes remain a long way off parity with men, their ministry hamstrung by the limitations of the 1987 measures, which have perhaps increased rather than diminished their frustration now that they are so nearly priests, but not quite.

For two years between 1985 and 1987 the Reverend Cathy Milford was, to all intents and purposes, the vicar of St Barnabas parish church in Heaton, Bradford. For a number of years she had been the curate, and when the vicar left it seemed entirely natural to all those connected with St Barnabas that Cathy should run the parish during the interregnum. It turned out to be a long one and when the new incumbent arrived Cathy was to face a sort of pain close to bereavement. It was assumed that her role would revert to that of a junior curate. In any other profession the only circumstances which could bring about such demotion would have involved some failure or misdemeanour on her part, but during Cathy's period in charge the congregation in Heaton had grown.

Cathy Milford's background is the same as that of many men her age who are now bishops. Her father was a distinguished Cambridge scientist; her own education was completed at Oxford with a first in History. Her interest in theology had developed in her teens at the Anglican boarding school where the history teacher who became her mentor told her that theology should be her subject, but the headmistress overruled the idea because 'girls didn't read things like theology'.

At Oxford, where she went on to study for a diploma in theology, she became involved with the Student Christian Movement, inspired by speakers like Father Huddleston and the social and ethical message of the Old Testament prophets. She wanted to pursue a career in the Church, but women had to be at least twenty-five years old to be considered and she was already coming up against closed doors.

For a while after Oxford she taught RE in multi-cultural Camden, and during this time married and had the first of her three children. She and her husband Nick, who teaches physics, then went out to Uganda to work in a Church of Uganda boarding school until the early seventies, when they were forced to leave by the Amin regime. But their experience with the Church in Uganda had been positive, and when they came back to the UK and Bradford they found the contrast with the Church of England sharp and disappointing.

Again, Cathy's inclination to join the ministry was thwarted and she went to work for the Marriage Guidance Council, but she was about to embark on the long process of entering the ministry, even though nobody would tell her how to go about it and, when she went straight to the then Bishop of Bradford, it was quite obvious that no effort would be made to help her, no support be given: 'I was advised against. They are very good at putting you off, not writing the letters that you need.'

Eventually she was accepted as a reader, a non-stipendiary office which would allow her to lead prayers, preach and take part in the pastoral work of the parish. Desperately short of money, she was unable to continue and had to take a paid job at a language centre for immigrant children in Bradford. Then, through the Marriage Guidance Council, she was offered an opportunity to spend a year in London studying in-depth marital and family therapy, all good training for the work of a priest.

'When I came back we had a new Bishop in Bradford and he asked me why I wasn't a deaconess. In eighteen months he had trained me – when the Church wants to get its skates on it can. I became a deaconess in June 1982.'

So what was the difference? Why did becoming a deaconess matter? 'It was recognition – and I got paid. It felt to be right. When people are willing to recognise change it happens, otherwise there is this shutter all the time and you can't get through.'

The curacy in Cathy's parish became vacant and she took the job along with enormous support from the congregation, who had known her in the beginning as one of them and watched her struggle into the ministry – a situation rarely parelleled by male clerics.

Cathy says she has always found general support from the congregation, though not understanding, because few people can grasp the politics of the Church. Her fellow clergy have generally regarded her as a colleague, and in Bradford this could hardly have been otherwise as the rural dean was an undergraduate with her at Oxford. As a result, she found her role expanding into other areas of community work: she became chairman of the local council of churches and until her ordination as a deacon in 1987, she was lay chairman of the deanery synod.

Then her moment came. The vicar at St Barnabas left and she took over, although legally the church wardens and the rural dean had charge of the parish. 'But as all three people involved were extremely busy they let it lapse to me,' she says. 'I had to drop all other interests to run the parish, but it was extremely rewarding and satisfying. A retired cleric came in for the Eucharist and others who didn't want to preach. It was all done with extreme courtesy, but I suppose we were fairly selective as to who we asked.'

'The Sunday morning parish Communion requires a lot of planning to make it go well and I was involved at a level I'd never achieved before. The congregation responded. There was no hassle, just lots of involvement. If I've got any gift it's in understanding the liturgy – relating what goes on in people's ordinary lives to the eternal. The whole thing needs to be dramatised, brought to life.' And it was at St Barnabas's, but two years on, that a new incumbent arrived to take over, a man considerably Cathy's junior in age and experience and instinctively inclined towards the 'paradigm of domination', as explained by Letty M. Russell, who writes about overcoming the Pinnacle Complex, which she describes as the greatest temptation for women and men in ministry. The 'paradigm of domination' inhibits the full participation of those at the bottom of the 'pyramid' in ministry and mission and divides ministry from laity. Russell says the model of authority is characterised by stereotypical masculine traits and that the Church has tried to ordain people to fulfil these characteristics.

'It was a badly thought out selection by the Church,' Cathy says of the St Barnabas appointment, 'although they must have said that I was part of a "package" with the job. The new vicar expected to treat me as a junior curate, doing only the things that he directed me to do. It led to arguments and terrible friction. I was so totally caught out. I couldn't believe anyone could be so stupid. I felt extremely bereft; it was almost like having a stillborn child. What really hurt was that the diocese would not recognise my situation. The bishop had died and the new bishop was not a person to take risks. It made me angry that the diocese couldn't see that I couldn't stay – they assumed that I would revert to being a junior curate. They could have left it longer because the parish was working so well – that was the way the Spirit was going and they couldn't see it.'

Six months after the event, Cathy's diocese did recognise the problem and set up a working party to devise a code of practice for parishes where there is a 'sitting' deacon; but for Cathy it was too late and in the summer of 1988 she and her family left Bradford. She went to Winchester, where she was offered the post of Adult Education Officer for the diocese – the sort of 'off-centre' job which is all that is available to ordained women seeking a career path through the Church of England.

'Other professions have been through the same thing, but the Church hasn't learnt from them. There is so much stupidity around and it's so tiring. The Church is surprised when women don't stay. It's all very confused,' she said. 'I do feel fairly depressed over the whole thing. The country is polarising politically and Synod is doing the same. Synod has gone sour. The central courtesy is going. I think they could draw back and stop women's ordination happening by 1992. The unity issue is fairly false. It's a scandal the way unity with the Nonconformists is ignored.

'The Church is afraid of openness to movement. It's unable to recognise where the Spirit is working. They want parishes to develop, but when they've got a woman there and it's working, they don't want to know.'

This has not been the experience of the Rev. Julie Childs, 'curate-in-charge' at St Mary's in Harpenden, Hertfordshire, also chair of MOW in her St Albans diocese. She, like every clergywoman, has come up against prejudice, but in Harpenden, one of the most affluent and Conservative towns in the country, she has won the day. People who know her call her Julie, otherwise, it's 'Vicar'.

A Christian all her life, she had leanings towards 'the cloth' in her teens, but immediately found opposition to the idea of women priests when she spoke to the curate in her home parish of Portsmouth: unequivocally he told her that the Church of England would never ordain women.

She did not pursue her calling then, but trained as an English and Drama teacher and went on to learn braille and the special skills needed to teach the blind. For several years she says she was completely absorbed by this work, but in the mid seventies again began to hanker after full-time work in the Church. By this time she was deputy head teacher at a school for severely physically handicapped children in Harpenden, but was increasingly needed at home to look after her elderly mother and decided to give up teaching and begin part-time training for the ministry. As she was about to complete this her mother died and an opportunity arose for a full-time stipendiary position at St Nicholas parish church in Harpenden. In practice, if not in name, she was the curate. Then the rector left to become a bishop and just before Christmas Julie took over his job for a year, even though there were two ordained men attached to the parish – a huge one with 1,100 on the electoral roll and more than 2,000 worshippers over the busy Christmas period.

'There were difficulties,' she says. 'Many people had reservations about the authority of women and some did try to undermine me: they would disagree over my plan of worship and I would be left out of meetings or find they had been fixed while I was away on holiday. But most people were very receptive, particularly when they saw how the Christmas services went totally smoothly.' She adds, ingenuously: 'My experience in rehearsing blind people for plays helped a great deal.'

In July 1986 a new rector came to St Nicholas and Julie worked with him during the hand-over period. Less than a year later she was ordained a deacon and asked to take charge of St Nicholas's daughter church, St Mary's. Her appointment was with the full approval of the church wardens and she now fulfils exactly the same function as a priest, except, of course, that she can't celebrate Holy Communion.

'The fact of my not being able to celebrate Communion is a matter of pain, and the current situation for women was highlighted when the new young curate came to St Nicholas's and was immediately able to celebrate. I could see the pain on a lot of people's faces in the congregation.'

Julie, like all the women clergy I have talked to, has stories to tell which have caused personal distress. Parents have refused to allow her to take weddings, even when the couple concerned have been prepared to accept her validity for the job. The bereaved have openly admitted to prejudice and demanded that a man be brought in for funerals. 'I prefer honest prejudice, but more often it's devious,' she says, adding: 'The vast majority of people will accept me and the experience of most women clergy is that people say all their doubts have gone during the course of a service.

'Once at a funeral a woman there was very "anti" and she thought she would not be able to go into the service when she saw me, but afterwards she said she realised she had been wrong all the years she had been against women. Women are as spiritual as men and the greatest need at the moment is for more women to go into full-time ministry.'

Julie admits that for a woman to succeed in a parish she has to have the support of her male colleagues, particularly of the vicar in charge, whose goodwill is essential. He can prevent her from carrying out pastoral work and many women have undergone extremely painful experiences where their vicar has maintained a traditionalist line: 'There are all sorts of assumptions based around the belief that men should take the lead; but there is also a great deal in society in general to be sorted out in this respect.'

A woman cannot have the 'cure of souls' as incumbent of a parish, and legally a woman cannot be 'curate-in-charge', yet in some dioceses the law is being 'worked around' and the bishops are now looking at how to enable women clergy to be officially acknowledged in the jobs they do. Julie Childs pointed out to me that increasingly the 'sits vac' columns of the *Church Times* carry ads for 'parish deacons' to be ministers-in-charge, and the very use of the term 'parish deacon' can refer only to women because men remain deacons for just one year before becoming priests, and during that period would be too young or inexperienced to have charge of a parish.

Julie feels that the women who take these jobs can find themselves in a powerful position, 'bridging' the gulf that has developed over the centuries between clergy and laity and bringing freshness to the ministry as well as change in the attitude towards women at the 'grass roots' — in the parishes, where the real change must happen. In her capacity as chair of MOW in the St Albans diocese, she plans to instigate a diocesan video showing women at work in the ministry and the reactions of their parishioners, particularly those who have had reservations about women clergy.

'The greatest band of resistance is from the elderly clergy who have grown up in a position of power and feel threatened by women, but it is also sad that so many women are against. There is the suggestion that women are not good at the practical side of organising a parish; at first I was always being asked if I had remembered this and that when I was planning things. And some people think we might show too much emotion, break down at funerals etc., although showing emotion need not be a sign of weakness — indeed, Jesus wept.'

For Julie there have been many occasions when her being a woman has proved an advantage in working with her flock on a one-to-one basis. Women will talk to her about deeply personal worries they would have found it impossible to mention to a man, but the limitations imposed on her ministry have been even more noticeable in such instances. 'As a woman I can't give a formal blessing or absolution of sins. It's so silly, this limitation, when all sorts of people go around saying 'God bless you' all the time.'

I asked her, just as I have many other women, why she doesn't just go ahead and do these things, and she said she won't because if women take canon law into their own hands there is a danger of upturning the whole authority of the Church. 'In a way we are prophets, and a false prophet will go against, will try to break, whereas a true prophet will work from within, niggling away at what has to be changed.

'If I was on a desert island or in a war and circumstances were desperate, I would have no hesitation in celebrating Holy Communion, blessing people and giving absolution.'

She believes that most people see her as a vicar now, even though she has been called 'deaconette', 'deaconese' and even once, 'arch-deaconess'. 'For most people, weddings, baptisms and funerals are what the vicar is for and I can do all these. In fact, Eucharistic worship has been at the centre of Anglicanism for only the last hundred years. Matins was before that, and if this was still the case would women now be vicars?'

In June 1988, as Cathy Milford was leaving her parish in Bradford and Julie Childs was settling into hers in Harpenden, I approached the vicar of my parish church in Royston, Hertfordshire, and asked him if a questionnaire on the women priests issue could be circulated among his parishioners. St John's is a lively and active church with a strong congregation. Royston is a country market town with a population of around 17,000 and one of the highest birth rates in the country, with many young couples having moved out from the London area to find cheaper housing. Worshippers at St John's are of all ages and broadly middle-class. For some years the ministry team has included a woman.

The questionnaire was as follows:

1 Do you think the vocation of priesthood would be diminished or enhanced if women were to be fully ordained?
2 Do you think the Church of England will suffer a serious split if women are fully ordained?
3 Do you think the ordination of women will finish the Church of England or make it stronger?
4 Have you, in another parish, experienced the ministry of a woman?
5 How would you feel if your vicar was a woman?
   i alarmed
   ii unconcerned
   iii pleased

There was also a space for further comment.

Of the 170 questionnaires distributed, 31 were returned. The vicar, the Rev. Patrick Bright, had predicted at the outset that only those who felt strongly either way would respond. As it turned out, 17 expressed themselves more or less in favour of women's ordination, but mostly with reservations, 7 were vehemently against and the remainder couldn't decide. Names were neither asked for nor given, but several of those against made a point of saying that they were women. One said she did not think a female vicar would be taken seriously, another that she would go elsewhere if St John's had a woman priest in charge, and a third wrote:

> As a woman I can find no overwhelming logical reasons against, but I don't *feel* that it would be right. If it must be so, careful selection of candidates is essential — may Heaven preserve us from women's libbers. It would be very ill-advised in that it would set back, perhaps for centuries, any closer union, either with Rome or the Orthodox Churches.

Another 'against' wrote:

> I feel that, on the whole, women's nature is too subjective and most women find it difficult to forget the work worries when they get home. I think it is also the wrong job to mix with husband and family. Most husbands would be unwilling to see their wives work the very long hours involved in the ministry — the norm is six days a week.
>
> I would be unhappy dealing with a woman at a personal level — especially in the sacraments — and would probably find a male priest nearby, but I am also anti-women doctors and I think these two dislikes come under the same heading.

Many of those in favour expressed the opinion that there would be a split in the Church, but few thought it would be long-term or serious. Most felt that the ordination of women would strengthen the Church, although few said they would be pleased to have a woman as their vicar. In most cases they ticked 'unconcerned'. In their comments, a large proportion indicated that they felt the Church should move with the times and that the subordinate role of women in the Church today was invidious. 'This is the twentieth century not the Middle Ages!' one person wrote. Another:

> I don't feel there is any reason why there should not be women priests, but I would not wish the movement to be pushed on merely to satisfy questions of equality at the risk of causing rifts within the Church. If the problem cannot be resolved without splitting the Church, then I feel that is a sad reflection on the Church, but I would rather we didn't risk everything for the sake of feminism. Rather, we should be considering the advantages that women priests, adding a new dimension, would bring and seek to

introduce them for the benefit of everybody, but if that is impossible then I would be happy to accept that.

'Personally,' wrote another, 'I would be very pleased to see the ordination of women, but I am well aware of the very strong feelings, particularly older people have (many of them women) against it.'

Perhaps the most heartfelt comment was: 'If the women were the clergy perhaps the men would be able to keep the children quiet.'

Finally, the story of Joyce Bennett, a woman who has run a very different sort of parish.

At the end of 1986 the Rev. Joyce Bennett was the only Anglican ordained woman priest living in England. There are more now, women like Patricia Pinkerton, whose story is told in Chapter Five, women who were ordained in the United States and have returned to England to fight it out on the real battleground of Anglicanism. But Joyce Bennett is different. She was accepted as an ordained woman here in the early 1980s, albeit as a deacon, not a priest, and licenced to minister despite her ordination having taken place in Hong Kong; and this at a time when fully ordained women from overseas were not even being granted deacon status by the Church of England.

The reason, it would seem, is that the Rev. Bennett had a USP (unique selling proposition): in the London diocese where she serves there is a substantial community of Chinese Anglicans, and they needed someone who spoke their language to lead their worship. Joyce Bennett, having spent the major part of her career in the Far East, was the ideal candidate, perhaps the only candidate, and in 1984 she joined the staff of St Martin-in-the-Fields, although without a salary.

What is more extraordinary is that she had become a minister in the diocese of the Bishop of London, and of course Dr Graham Leonard is the most powerful opponent of women's ordination in this country.

Joyce Bennett was brought up in the Church, but as a child never imagined herself becoming a vicar. She studied history at Westfield College but felt that God was calling her elsewhere, and in the 1940s she went out to Hong Kong with the Church Missionary Society. There she met the Rev. Florence Tim Oi Li, the first Anglican woman to be ordained to the priesthood, although for reasons of expediency rather than of theological equality.

In 1962 Joyce Bennett followed her lead and became ordained to the diaconate, although it would be another nine years before her full entry to the priesthood when in November 1971 the Far Eastern diocese undertook the first female ordination to the priesthood of modern times. The Chinese Synod's decision to allow this had been made by an overwhelming majority and yet women were not to be ordained at the same service as men. To have allowed this would, in the eyes of the Church, have given a false impression of women's position within it.

Despite her ordination, Joyce Bennett did not take a parish but continued her teaching work as the principal of a large secondary school for girls, although she always considered that the thousand-plus pupils in her care were her parish: 'In many parts of the world now the old parish system doesn't exist in the same way,' she told me. 'The school was an opportunity to minister.'

In 1983 she decided to retire and felt that she was being called back to England to help with the campaign for the ordination of women. 'A lot of the Church of England is very fossilised. I felt it was important to be here. I felt I could help in some way. The Church here does not seem to understand what has gone on overseas. The Holy Spirit has spoken and been received abroad.'

She lives now in the village of her childhood, Prestwood in Buckinghamshire, in a small, modern terraced house on a new housing estate with her Chinese god-daughter Mary. Visits to the parish which she serves in the centre of London are frequent and very time-consuming: 'The other Saturday I went on a two-and-a-half-hour journey to bless a new flat for one of our congregation, then a two-and-a-half-hour journey back. This is an example of my pastoral work; another is being rung up by funeral directors who can't communicate with Chinese – wonderful opportunities.'

In Hong Kong the Rev. Bennett never showed herself as a priest in outward dress; she says she never wore a dog collar, but has been persuaded to do so here, and now feels this is important. She is asked if she is one of the new deacons and says: 'No, I am a priest from Hong Kong.' But how is a woman priest from Hong Kong received by the Bishop of London with all his theological prejudice against ordaining women?

'I have been robed in the sanctuary at St Martin-in-the-Fields with the Bishop. He could not produce a male priest to work with the Chinese congregation. But in July 1984 when I first met him he had not taken the trouble to find out about me. He had assumed that I was there to confound him, but once we got talking it became clear that he was very pastoral and concerned. I've never really talked to him properly since. He's always rushing off to the next thing.'

When I asked her about Dr Leonard's comment on how he would feel at the sight of a woman at the altar, she said: 'The Bishop of London has never embraced me.'

This seems to be true in more than the physical sense, because the Bishop has now found a male priest to work with his Chinese flock and the man in question, unlike Joyce Bennett, will be paid a stipend.

Like Cathy Milford, Joyce Bennett, throughout the five years of organising worship in her parish, has always had to have an ordained man present to preside at the Eucharist. 'We have a male priest there to cover ourselves, but I say the liturgy in Chinese and all members of the congregation accept me as a priest. When everything is going on in Chinese, the fact that a man up there is saying something in English – well, nobody takes any notice.

'I think it is very sad that the Church of England has moved so slowly and not understood changes in society. We are losing younger people because of it. If you wish to work in an historic Church – as people lived 200 years ago – that's a museum and it shouldn't be like that. It is a living faith.'

She will continue ministering at St Martin's, helping the new priest. She says she has no bitterness or anger over the way things are, only sadness, and that since returning to the UK she has not really felt at home in the Church of England: 'We didn't have this fight in Hong Kong – it only builds up walls. Instead, we should be breaking them down. The whole serving role of the priest needs to be re-emphasised – emphasis that women might well give.'

FIVE

Who is making all the fuss?

'There are two places in the world where discrimination is still legal, in South Africa with Apartheid and in England with the Church.' (GGK, MOW's advertising agency, *Campaign*, November 1987)

The two principal organisations making most of the fuss over whether or not women should be admitted to the priesthood are the Movement for the Ordination of Women (MOW) formed in 1979, and Women Against the Ordination of Women (WAOW) formed in 1986. Both claim membership in excess of 4,000, together with the support of other church groups for and against – among them, Women in Theology (for) and the Association for the Apostolic Ministry (against). Both MOW and WAOW have their troops in the parishes and dioceses marshalling support, and their lobbyists within the power structure of the Church of England, but it is MOW that has enlisted the help of the 'professionals'.

Advertising executive Kitty O'Hagan has set about doing for MOW what Saatchis did for the Conservative Party, and similarly, the fact that the Movement for the Ordination of Women had taken on an ad agency (GGK, based in the West End of London) proved a bigger news item than the cause itself. The 'fuss' was to become professionally orchestrated with provocative poster campaigns depicting attractive young clerics of both sexes, placed side by side with a message full of poignancy, pathos and that touch of piety

66

symbolised by the dog collar. It is just sufficient to separate the product from the consumer goods more commonly handled by GGK, reported in the advertising industry's *Campaign* magazine as having been given the task of ridding the Church of England of sexual discrimination.

Kitty O'Hagan has spent the past twenty years researching how women respond to advertising, and as far as the Church is concerned she feels that it is women who are the decision-makers in whether or not a family goes to Sunday services.

'In the past women have not readily respected other women, but the majority don't feel this way any more. The change has come about in the last two to three years. The balance has tipped.'

The association between GGK and MOW began after Kitty, GGK's planning director, heard one of the leaders of the Movement, Margaret Webster, talking at the City Women's Network in London. 'She's a cracker — sensible, stimulating. She made the analogy that women trying to get into the Church was like women trying to get into management. She referred to the *Church Times* as the 'trade press'. I was interested and motivated and I offered to help. I'm not an actively religious person; I don't go to church, but I probably would if there was a woman priest. I think they would improve their 'ratings' if they let women in — but maybe they don't want more people. If they want people to buy their product, why do they resist appealing to women?'

In taking on the MOW account, which in billing terms is worth nothing to GGK — 'the thinking is for free' — Kitty realised that the issue had to be taken out of the world of religion and into the real world, as she puts it. She felt that the combination of women and religion conjured up images of peculiar, shaven-headed, asexual, nun-like creatures, and that one of her tasks was to put hair on the head, to change the public perception of women in the Church and reveal them as ordinary and normal.

'MOW badly needed help in communication. They thought that people understood that women could only become deacons, but the general public was confused; becoming deacons sounded equal to full ordination or even more impressive than being a priest. We had to make the distinction clear and make the whole issue one of sexual discrimination.'

The poster campaign that ensued at the end of 1987 went out to the parishes, to the grass roots of the Church. It pictured two deacons, the Rev. Nigel Davies and the Rev. Jayne Tyrer, both with diplomas in theology, both in clerical garb. The message was that after twelve months' probation Nigel would progress to become a priest and in time, perhaps a bishop, even an archbishop, while Jayne had already reached the pinnacle of her career and would remain a deacon unless the rules could be changed. The further message was that Jayne, who in any other employment would be able to claim a breach of the Equal Opportunities Act, had no recourse to law because the Church of England was, and still is, excluded from the Act.

Kitty O'Hagan put out a press release to coincide with the initial poster campaign. The heading was 'Her Sexuality Gets in the Way of Her Job', and pictured Ann Easter. The copy capitalised on the Bishop of London's now famous, some would say, infamous reply when asked on BBC Radio 4 whether he feared that our idea of God would be affected by seeing a woman at the altar. He said that his instinct would be to take her in his arms, and that 'sexuality is built into human life'.

The next paragraph of the release stated: 'Of course, the question that begs to be asked is, what about the female congregation's sexual feelings towards the male clergy?'

The effect of the release was to extend coverage of MOW's cause beyond the columns of the *Guardian*: 'Now they were in the *Mail* as well – everyone was interested,' Kitty says. 'Going public about it has lifted it to a big issue with public opinion behind it.'

This is the sort of statement with which Margaret Hood, a founder member of WAOW – Women Against the Ordination of Women – takes issue. WAOW was formed on 23 April 1986 to make it clear to the world that MOW does not represent the whole of public opinion and, more specifically, the opinion of a large number of women in the Anglican Communion. Margaret and her fellow founders were highly irritated by what seemed to them an assumption on the part of MOW that no woman in the Church of England could possibly disagree with them: 'The MOW propaganda at that time was that the only objectors to women's ordination were priests worried about losing their foothold in the Church. This made me very cross. I was in contact with a lot of women – through the Church Union, the Prayer Book Society – and none of us wanted women to be priests.'

WAOW, like MOW (and the Church of England itself, for that matter), encompasses a broad spectrum of belief, and the women against, although united in their opposition, have starkly varying views on why they are so opposed. Margaret Hood is a self-proclaimed feminist, a working mother, matron of a large hospital in Gloucestershire. Brought up in the Anglican Church, but in a somewhat 'piggy in the middle' position between a mother whose preference was for Ann Easter's 'smells and bells' of the High Church, and a father who was at the opposite end in the Low protestant pews, she says it was a wonderful example of the tremendous breadth of understanding within Anglicanism and never gave rise to the slightest tension. Her own inclination is towards the High Church, and in her marriage one has a similar situation to that of her parents. Her husband, a policeman, is Low Church and bored by the issue of women priests.

Her interest began twenty years ago when she was a student nurse and heard Dr Margaret Hewitt, prominent amongst those against the ordination of women, explaining why. Dr Hewitt accepted the invitation to chair the 2,000-strong WAOW some eighteen years later, at its formation following a meeting in London between women and men 'against'.

'There was a powerhouse of anti-women-priest women there,' Margaret Hood says. 'At the end of the meeting it was clear that the men "against" felt totally unable to face or challenge MOW. They would be called male chauvinist pigs and accused, as mere men, of being incapable of understanding.'

From the start, WAOW decided to limit its membership to practising Anglican churchgoers, a criterion they claim is not the case with MOW membership. Every woman at the London meeting realised that they knew of at least ten other women against, and from there WAOW quickly built up its numbers, encompassing women who, unlike Margaret Hood, believe that their place is in the home; women who want to be led, as Peter Bruinvels has put it; and those, like Margaret, who cite purely theological reasons for their objection. Her belief is that the roles of the sexes were clearly set out when Christ came to earth as a man, and that God used woman in a unique way because Christ's entire and complete human nature was derived from her. She believes that to 'fudge' this distinction between the sexes would reduce the Virgin Mary's part in the proceedings to a base sexual level.

Following such an argument is not easy, and indeed there have been times when Margaret has faltered herself, but she has come through her doubts and is even more convinced that what she believes is right. In a pamphlet published by the Association for the Apostolic Ministry she states:

> The freedom that modern feminism promises is an illusion because it offers only equality with men. Christian feminism offers another freedom because it asserts that woman is different from man. It establishes her unique relationship with God and creation. I believe that this makes priesthood of women unnecessary. It makes the priesthood of women pointless and meaningless.

Elaborating on the inevitable connection between feminism and the ordination of women, she goes on to write:

> The ugliest side of feminism is its preoccupation with achieving status and success. All the women who have gained access to important positions in industry, politics, commerce and the professions state unequivocally that they have not only had to work very hard to be accepted but that they have had to show exceptional qualities. And whatever qualities were required to gain admission have also had to be maintained at that high standard if progress and promotion are to be ensured. To see the priesthood as another area where certain skills and qualifications will permit entry is to demean the sacred office of priesthood. It is naive to refuse to see the corrupting influence modern feminism is having on the Church.

Speaking in the living-room of her Cotswolds cottage, she told me: 'I believe that what I want for women in the Church is better than being a priest, but I think I have a different concept of priesthood to others. I think it will be catastrophic for the Church of England to think any further about the ordination of women until we have had the most serious and widest possible exploration into the connection between the growth of feminism and the call to ordain women. The danger is that the character of the Church of England will be so altered that it will no longer exist as we know it. I am beginning to ask myself whether the Church of England is dying a very slow death because it has served its use in the history of Christendom.'

Now, this is strong stuff and maybe the Church has been right in its 'oppression' of women if they are to be instrumental in its downfall. Margaret seems to be saying that the political factions of the Church are in danger of joining forces in its slaughter. In the pamphlet mentioned above, she talks about the Church of England at war: 'The struggle for ordination has become a bitter contest and the women who have been ordained have the air of victors who have won the battle in their sector and are urging on the generals in the rest of this theatre of war.'

WAOW feels that MOW has been losing ground in recent years, that the movement has reached its ceiling of support, that there has been a 'sea change' because MOW no longer claims to be speaking for the women of the Church.

'I have had members of MOW shouting at me from the back of a hall – "You, Margaret Hood, have ratted on your own sex." Thousands of women in the Church of England are no longer afraid to voice their opposition, but this has brought about a change in MOW's approach, a new one that is destructive, whereas the previous approach was only irritating. They are saying that there is no argument against women priests – that such an argument cannot exist because every argument can be counter-balanced. I am not taken seriously. I am not considered a serious opponent. It is terrifying, and inevitably there comes a time when you have to ask which side is totally misguided. To say we have no theological argument eventually makes you doubt whether you actually have — whether you exist at all. Do I exist as a current member of the Church, or am I just somebody who is hanging on to outdated antediluvian beliefs? It seems I can be "disappeared", told to pack up my spiritual bags and go elsewhere.'

Margaret does not have an answer to the problem of women priests, but she feels that the Church may draw back from the issue because 'it is leading us into terrifying spiritual deserts where we have to ask what is the purpose of male and female; I don't believe that anyone has ever been there before and the image of the desert throughout the Bible is such that we don't go there voluntarily'.

WAOW now has over 4,000 members in the UK and branches in Canada, Australia and the United States. There are members in their teens and members in their nineties, and support is growing at the rate of 75–100 enquiries per week.

It is run by a central committee with representatives in each of the 44 dioceses of England. Action varies from diocese to diocese, according to what is appropriate in each case, but mostly the message is delivered through Mothers' Union-type meetings with a clear directive that there must be no 'undignified protest of the sort that does not befit Christian women'. There must be no marching, no disturbance and absolutely no lobbying of priests. Prayer, persuasion, example and discussion are the order of the day, although much bitterness is evident, particularly in America from where WAOW receives many letters written by those who say they wish there had been a similar organisation there before it was too late. They say 'schism' is already a reality in the Episcopalian Church; that those who have chosen to go with what are termed the 'continuing' churches are viewed as occupying little pockets of effete traditionalism; and that those who have remained in the mainstream where women are priests have experienced social and spiritual ostracism — some have capitulated through loneliness and misery, but they still try to avoid services conducted by women.

A common response from those in favour of ordaining women to those against is that first-hand experience of women in ministry can bring about conversion, but many in WAOW find this seemingly reasonable and humane suggestion the most infuriating of all the arguments 'for'. They claim that it is entirely missing their point, based on implicit belief in the apostolic succession which would be totally destroyed if women were to become not only priests, but by inevitable progression, bishops.

There are those in WAOW who say they will no longer go to church if women are admitted to the priesthood in England, but will live, broken-hearted, beyond the sacraments. 'I would spend the rest of my life grieving over the greatest loss that I could have,' says Margaret Hood. 'I would lose the ability to communicate on a deeply personal level with Christ because I don't think I could survive outside the Church. I need the sacraments to nourish my spiritual life.'

'I am not a member of the Church of England by mistake. I chose to belong to this branch of the Christian Church and I want to hand on to my children the inestimable riches of my spiritual heritage, not the poverty of an institution almost destroyed by internecine warfare.'

The Bishop of London has warned that the Church of England will break up if women become priests. Margaret Hood says: 'I am a terminal-care nurse by profession. If we ordain women I will have a similar approach to the Church. I will look on it as in a terminal phase – all active intervention will have ceased. I can only give help to enable dying with dignity and without pain.'

The day before I visited Margaret Hood, I had been to another house, in the village of Cuddesdon near Oxford. There, in a living-room which contained, among other things, an antique lectern, a 'bishop's' chair, an opal-eyed cat named Isaac and an enormous house-trained rabbit suffering from a head cold, I spent several hours talking to Pat Pinkerton, or the Reverend Patricia Pinkerton, or Reverend Mother, as her parishioners in California chose to call her.

Pat is British and has come home to join the fight. Her story is a sad one. Having suffered considerable pain in her personal life, won through and achieved ordination in the States, she seems, to the outside observer, to have thrown it all away and chosen to start again in a climate of hostility and heartache.

She left England for America in the early 1960s, married to part of the 'brain drain'. Like Margaret Hood, she was a nurse by profession but her career in California was cut short by a serious back problem. This was just the beginning of a terrible time to come in which she lost her husband and then her children, taken from her because she had no money and was to be declared an 'unfit' mother.

Having hit rock bottom, she had to find a new identity in herself in order to climb out of her despair. She had returned to the Church and decided to study for a Master's degree in art and church history with particular emphasis on cathedral life and the liturgy. Eventually, she was to 'major' on monasticism, and during this time began to contemplate joining an order; but this was not to be the right route for her, as became clear when she met and married her second husband. Yet the strong sense of vocation remained, throwing her into a turmoil of doubt because she didn't feel particularly 'worthy' as a divorced, albeit remarried, person. Then something extraordinary happened.

Pat divides religious people into two categories, 'feelers' and 'thinkers', and as a 'feeler' herself she is open to symbolism, signs and, on this singular occasion, a vision. Kneeling before the altar, ready to receive the Host, she felt what seemed like blood running down her face. She looked up at the Cross and saw the kneeling figure of the Magdalen. The hot, heavy liquid on her face was not blood, but tears, but the kneeling figure she saw was a vision.

At this time in the Episcopal Church, during the mid-seventies, women had begun to be ordained illegally. Pat applied to be trained as a deacon, the vision having left her with a clear feeling that she was called to the ordained ministry. She studied for a few years, underwent psychological evaluation and when the moment came for her admission to orders, was turned down. 'It was another devastation,' she says. 'I was told to sit in the pews for a year and not allowed to do anything in the ministry.' By the end of that year she was angry, but it had given her time to realise that it was not the diaconate she wanted but priesthood. She approached her parish priest and was told that this was the decision the committee that had turned her down for the diaconate had been waiting for her to make. She went on to be legally ordained and was asked to set up a new mission in San José in the diocese of El Camino Real. Within two years she had seventy parishioners attending services in a converted schoolroom.

Reaction to her calling and ordination has of course been mixed, especially as she was the first woman to hold cure in her diocese. She has been asked if she's a lesbian, as if she had to be to want to be ordained; and: 'If you're a priest how come you wear make-up?' was an early question. Pat's response is the same now as it was then, that the best way she can relate to anyone – from a queen to a harlot – is to be, openly and obviously, the twentieth-century woman that she is.

'People have always been responsive to me in accepting me in the parishes,' she says. 'On the day I was ordained I was given a gift from someone who had been against women priests but who had changed his mind. I think God puts women in places where there are people against, where there will be the chance to minister to them and change their minds.' But this is not always the case, and on one occasion Pat was present, though not presiding, at the Eucharist and a would-be recipient refused to accept the bread and the wine from the hands of the bishop because it was felt that the mere presence of a woman at the altar invalidated the whole proceedings.

Such occurrences were, in Pat's American experience, the exception. The equivalent of MOW's sexual discrimination poster described at the beginning of this chapter is, in the Episcopalian Church, a picture of an altar with the legend 'Where women stand in the Episcopalian Church'. Coming back to England, it was a different story.

In the summer of 1987 Pat told her husband that she felt compelled to return home and help MOW. 'I just couldn't go on pulling a good salary ($35,000 per annum) in California and being a vicar, knowing that in England women could not do this.' Her husband agreed straight away and at the same time decided that he

too wished to become a priest. At first everything seemed to fall
into place. The Pinkertons were to come to Cuddesdon, where Pat
had been offered the chaplaincy at Ripon College and curacy of the
parish, traditionally offices which go together. At the same time, her
husband would study for the priesthood at the college.

'It was like finding the Grail,' says Pat. 'Ripon, the last bastion of
male dominance.' But first there was to be delay and then outright
rejection, straight from Lambeth Palace.

In order to take up her new position at Cuddesdon Pat needed to
be licensed as a deacon by the Church of England. After months of
waiting, during which time her husband had completed his first term
at the College, she received a letter from the Archbishop of
Canterbury, dated 4 January 1988, in which he said he had given
careful consideration to her request to be 'licensed' but had to
withhold his permission until there was more support in the Church
of England for the ministry of women ordained overseas.*

The Archbishop's refusal to 'license' Pat was devastating enough,
but there was to be a further blow for the Pinkertons when it came
to light that they had both been divorced from their first partners.
By re-marrying, Pat's husband had disqualified himself from ordination and was never to begin his second term at Ripon.

'Staying in Cuddesdon is like looking through a window at a
party to which you are not invited,' Pat said, two months after
receiving the Archbishop's letter. At the time she was waiting to
hear from John Yates of Gloucester, Margaret Hood's bishop, and a
MOW supporter: there was a chance that she could be licensed as a
lay person to work in a more sympathetic diocese than Oxford,
whose bishop had declined a meeting to discuss her plight. But why
stay in England at all? Why not go back to America where she
could resume her ministry, in charge of her own parish, legally
entitled to celebrate the Eucharist? The suggestion has been made,
but Pat is convinced that she has to stay. 'Change is coming about
because of my difficult situation – the unusual nature of it – people
are being forced to think about it all. There is no question of going

---

* At the end of 1988 the Rev. Patricia Pinkerton was granted permission to be
licensed to the diaconate.

back.' She says this believing that the change is not going to take place as soon as MOW hopes, that the 1990s will not be the time in England: 'We will get much further with the male ego if changes are gradual,' she says, 'and we have to prove to clergy wives that we are not going to be in the sacristy, that we are not going to be raping their husbands.'

Until such time as all the proof is accepted, Pat has said that she will not celebrate the Eucharist. Like Margaret Hood, she has said that this will be her sacrifice: 'I have refused all the invitations. It would be so easy to nip off celebrating here, celebrating there, in people's houses. I'd love it, but I have to make this sacrifice, to show how I understand the hurting. It is the ultimate sacrifice, giving up that which is most precious to me, but to go back on it would be like giving up something for Lent and then cheating on it.'

Pat feels there is a need for the strident women, like those in Philadelphia in the seventies who pushed and pushed and won the day, but she says she cannot be like that herself, although she would chain herself to railings if it would help. Her view is that God gave women wiles and meant them to be used.

'I allowed myself to be with women who are convinced of their calling or of the authenticity of a calling for their sisters,' states the Rev. Donald Edgar, a convert to MOW. 'I have moved from opposing to supporting the ordination of women. In allowing myself to be with women in their quest for recognition, I experienced also the Church that "sits down with" the poor and the weak. It is in this environment that there are the seeds of tomorrow's Church. It is not a hierarchical Church, but one where what and who God ordains is put at the service of the poor, the weak; and these include women who aren't granted their full status as inheritors of the kingdom.'

Perhaps the Rev. Edgar was experiencing the 'wiles' that Pat Pinkerton describes. Certainly, there are many Anglicans who have similarly changed camps after witnessing women in ministry. The Bishop of Gloucester has said to Margaret Hood that if only she allowed herself to experience a woman in action she might alter

her opinion, but this is the sort of argument that most provokes
those against. Theologically, they say that it is missing the point
whether or not women can be good in the pulpit, in the parish,
at the altar. The basis of their argument is enshrined in the
tradition of apostolic succession, a men-only tradition written in
the Scriptures.

With this tradition central to their opposition to women's ordination, the Association for the Apostolic Ministry was set up in the
mid-eighties. It was founded by the 150-year-old Church Union,
historical defender of Anglican clergy persecuted for 'Romish' practices, and still working today for union with the Catholics.

The Church Union, AAM and WAOW, together represent a formidable, even sinister block of opposition to MOW, and their methods
are winning ground. In England and elsewhere in the Anglican
Communion they are gaining Synod seats in order to influence
diocesan reaction to the legislation drafted for women's ordination.
By taking this 'grass roots' approach they are developing a network
of opposition that will undermine any General Synod attempt to
legalise women as priests.

Arthur Leggatt, joint secretary of AAM, which with WAOW has
more than 5,000 members, predicts that ultimately MOW will fail;
that the vote will go against. 'Looking at the previous voting
pattern, with less than the required two-thirds majority in favour in
the House of Clergy and this hardly reached in the House of Laity,
we think the move will fail,' he told me. 'There are new members in
both Houses who are known to be against, and even in the House
of Bishops there is growing concern about schism.'

In AAM's leaflet 'Why We Must Say No', produced in the mid-
eighties, the 40 per cent of Clergy and 30 per cent of Laity who do
not believe that a woman can be a priest are cited as an additional
argument to that of theological tradition. For them, women's ordination can never be valid, sacraments administered by a woman would
be meaningless. As a parish priest a woman could not claim the
loyalty of all in the parish, or rely on being accepted as a fellow
priest by all the clergy; and if she were to become a bishop she
could not expect to receive the full allegiance of the diocese.

AAM propounds that the Church is presently the victim in a society which confuses equality with sameness and that pressure to ordain women is simply conformity to the world's current values. It suggests that while the debate about women and the priesthood continues, other possibilities of ministry for women are hindered and unexplored.

At heart, 'schism' is AAM's greatest fear. Born out of the Church Union with its long history of campaigning for Unity with Rome and the Orthodox Churches, it is anathema to AAM that disunity should happen *within* the Church of England. Their leaflet states:

> If the Church of England were to ordain women, some – we
> cannot speculate how many – of the laity and clergy would feel
> obliged to leave, to take refuge in some other Church which
> remained faithful to Scripture and Tradition. Others – again we
> cannot speculate how many – might try and form their own
> 'continuing Anglican' Church, taking with them as many bishops,
> priests and lay people as they could, with as many of their buildings
> and endowments as they were allowed to. Others, determined not
> to break away from the Church of England but convinced that
> women cannot be ordained, would be forced into a 'ghetto' of
> parishes where women were not permitted to officiate as priests,
> relying on the determination of priests and Church councils making
> full use of the 'rights of conscience' that would have to be conceded
> by the General Synod.
>
> Such things have already happened in Canada and the United
> States; we do not have to approve of this or that course of action
> – adopted by people desperate to remain true to the Faith and
> Order of the Church – to foresee that they would happen here:
> time-wasting synodical procedures, distracting the Church from more
> important tasks; expensive and unseemly legal actions in the courts;
> wrangles over property, and rights to hold office and receive
> emoluments; 'rebel' parishes defying their bishops. These things
> have happened elsewhere; we do not want them here.

Even so, they look likely to happen if women become priests in the Church of England. It was reported in the *Church Times* towards the end of 1988 that more than a thousand priests and lay people were now ready to break away and form a Continuing Church of England.

The report stated that groups had been set up in twenty counties, taking guidelines from the Anglican Catholic Church in America. In addition, a group known as the Epiphany Fellowship is reported to be flourishing. Members are men who believe that they have a vocation, but who have been turned down as ordinands, owing, they claim, to their traditionalist beliefs. Membership also encompasses those who have felt unable to offer themselves in the present climate of the established Church. The embryo Continuing Church has not promised to ordain all of them, but says it is confident of finding a bishop to do so for those selected.

This chapter would be incomplete without an interview with one of the strongest activists in MOW, a mother of the movement and yet a woman who does not seek ordination for herself. Monica Furlong is a self-proclaimed radical and few would disagree with this. Within MOW she represents those who foresee a rocky road ahead and aim to tackle each obstacle head-on. She was among the demonstrators early on, in 1980, who gatecrashed an ordination ceremony in St Paul's and held up banners demanding women's ordination.

'It brought the issue to public attention,' she says. 'MOW really got started after that. We now have between four and five thousand members, which is extraordinary for a church organisation; mostly about twelve hundred is the limit.'

She became MOW's moderator in 1982, serving three years before handing over to her less radical successor, Diana McClatchey, who represents the 'softly, softly' faction within the movement.

Monica Furlong, a successful writer of novels, non-fiction and many articles, was born of an Irish Catholic father and a partly Jewish mother. She was brought up an Anglican but had a conversion experience when she was nineteen which has kept her in the Church of England ever since, although she is a regular worshipper with the St Hilda Community in London, the breakaway group which has an ordained woman from overseas preside at Communion services. St Hilda's is anathema to many in the mainstream of the Church of England; it engenders huge resentment and is generally

considered to be unlawful. Yet it comprises only about 200 people
and average weekly attendance is around just sixteen or seventeen.

Monica Furlong, and those who worship at these 'illegal' services,
want a massive change of heart to take place in the Church that
they love. 'What sort of Church do I want? I would like a Church
that is far more realistic – not so harsh, especially with people who
don't fit in. I would like a Church where people can speak the truth
about themselves and feel accepted and loved.' She speaks of a huge
well of prejudice and fear in the Church as it stands today, and sees
the women priests issue as a means of bringing out all the skeletons
that haunt it: 'the hatred towards women throughout Christianity,
so much repressed sexuality, women always getting the blame for
luring men into sex, then the extreme idealisation of women like the
Virgin Mary, who are only OK if they don't have any sex. We are
touching the deep, frightened places.

'And you can't leave Adam and Eve out of this: the harm of the
Adam and Eve story is one of the skeletons in the closet. I find the
story rather wonderful, but, of course, we didn't hear it from Eve's
point of view, did we. And by continually speaking of God as
"Him" we have created an impression that God is a man and
therefore if you are a man you are closer to "Him".'

She goes on to cite witchcraft – or, rather, the Christian persecution of women as witches – as another skeleton to be taken out of
the Church's closet and examined, so that it can be seen as further
evidence of men's fear of women and their apparent need to keep
them under firm control. Despite all this, she still feels deeply
attracted by some aspects of Christianity, particularly the central
pattern of crucifixion and resurrection: 'It is the best description of
human experience I have come across; everyone gets crucified and
resurrected.'

Talking about the priesthood, she would like to see changes in
how it is perceived, with the priest drawing out other people rather
than being the star turn, although she adds that many priests are
already working this way. She sees the issue of women's ordination
as just the tip of the iceberg, 'the bit you see', and part of something
a great deal bigger. 'I am not that interested in women's ordination

— I am interested in the Church having a different attitude towards women — in employment, over pornography, rape, all these things which they couldn't care less about at present. There is a steady drain of young women dropping out of the Church, and there will be many more if ordination is not given the go-ahead by 1992. Yet this state of affairs could not go on if women did not allow it to happen. Women account for 60 per cent of congregations and they could withhold their money from the collection — they could say they were going to keep it until women were ordained. They could also refuse to clean the churches. Women have always been told it is Christ-like to sacrifice yourself and therefore they have become masochistic in the Church and made sacrifices they shouldn't.'

Monica Furlong believes the ordination of women is a bigger issue than it might seem. She says it affects the whole of society. 'Breaking this last bastion is very important. It means re-thinking what masculine and feminine roles are, throwing everything back into the melting pot — more so with the priesthood than any other job in society.'

Writing in the *Guardian*, the day after the General Synod voted in favour of women priests in July 1988, she said it seemed that for the first time in over sixty years of debate the issue was being given the seriousness it deserved, even to the point of suggesting some repentance from men in the Church over their past attitudes towards women. But when I spoke to her she said she felt there would have to be an extraordinary change of heart for women to be ordained by 1992, although she added: 'The vast majority of Anglicans couldn't care one way or another.'

SIX

Synod — is it dodging the issue and blaming Rome?

An article in the *Sun* newspaper in 1987 headed 'Unholy Row in Church' stated: 'The Church is too important to be left to the clergy to tear apart. The old Church of England tradition of compromise is dead, and civil war threatens over this one issue.'

The 'one issue' referred to was, of course, the ordination of women, said by one bishop to be 'the most controversial decision the Church of England has been faced with since the Reformation'. The *Sun* article was suggesting that the freedom given to the Church in the 1970s by Prime Minister James Callaghan, to choose its own bishops, should be rescinded and the ancient powers of the Crown restored in a bid to bring back balance and sanity. Whether or not the writer of this piece was looking for a decision in favour of ordaining women to the priesthood, or against, is unclear, and maybe this was not his point: perhaps he was trying to say that what was important was decision itself and an end to the rowing.

It was in 1975 that the General Synod, the governing body of the Church of England, decided that it could find no fundamental objections to the ordination of women. This was more than thirty years after the ordination of Florence Tim Oi Li in the Far East, and a year after the 'illegal' ordination of eleven women in the United States. By the end of the decade, Canada and New Zealand were legally ordaining women and the irregular ordinations in America had been officially approved.

In 1982 the England Synod voted to introduce legislation to ordain women as deacons, which came into effect in 1987. Within a year Kenya and Uganda were ordaining their women as priests. The following year, 1984, in England the General Synod voted in favour of the Bishop of Southwark's motion to bring forward legislation to permit the ordination of women to the full priesthood – voted in favour, but not by the overall two-thirds majority required for major change. The House of Bishops led the way with 87 per cent in favour, while the House of Laity had 63 per cent and the House of Clergy only 57 per cent.

By July 1988, when the issue came forward again, voting had changed and, although a majority was still in favour, support had dropped to 57 per cent in the Houses of Bishops and Clergy, and 59 per cent in the House of Laity. The vote concerned draft legislation, which, in its final form would have to win the overall two-thirds majority before progressing beyond Synod for Parliamentary approval in the Lords and the Commons, and, finally, Royal Assent. But between July and November 1988 a staggering 465 amendments were received by the Synod office, all of them submitted by Synod members.

There are those within the Church who say that it is impossible to govern by Synod and that this is the reason why the Church of England is in disarray, while the Roman Catholics and the new Fundamentalist churches are thriving under dictatorial rule in an almost post-egalitarian age. Whether the Synod critics are right or wrong, the difference between the government of the Church of England and that of the Church of Rome is fundamental when it comes to the issue of women priests. Both Churches are keen for unity, but the ordination of women stands between them and, while the one Church is attempting to resolve the question by democratic means, the other claims a divine autocracy which would seem to make debate difficult, if not impossible. Nevertheless, there is much goodwill on both sides, a lot of work has been done in the shape of an international commission, joint reports, and correspondence between the Pope and the Archbishop of Canterbury. Even so, the only conclusion to be reached from reading letters which have passed between Canterbury and Rome is that every time another branch of the Anglican Communion allows women to be ordained, the wedge between the two Churches is driven in further.

Writing to the Archbishop in December 1984, the Pope said:

I know that Your Grace is well aware of the position of the Catholic Church and of the theological grounds which lead her to maintain it; indeed I am grateful that, in the recent debate in the General Synod of the Church of England, you referred to the implications of this question for Anglican relations with the Catholic and Orthodox Churches. But the outcome of that debate prompts me to reaffirm with all brotherly frankness the continuing adherence of the Catholic Church to the practice and principles so clearly stated by Pope Paul VI.

With his well-known affection for the Anglican Communion and his deep desire for Christian unity, it was with profound sadness that Pope Paul VI contemplated a step which he saw as introducing into our dialogue 'an element of grave difficulty', even 'a threat'. Since that time we have celebrated together the progress towards reconciliation between our two Communions. But in those same years the increase in the number of Anglican Churches which admit, or are preparing to admit, women to priestly ordination constitutes, in the eyes of the Catholic Church, an increasingly serious obstacle to that progress.

A year later the Archbishop replied:

The Churches of the Anglican Communion and the Roman Catholic Church are fully committed to the quest for full ecclesiastical unity . . . The question of admission of women to the ministerial priesthood is a divisive matter not only between our Churches but also within them. It is surely a sign of both the seriousness and the maturity of Anglican–Roman Catholic relations that we can exchange letters on a subject surrounded by controversy . . . In this fraternal spirit I am bound to report that – although Anglican opinion is itself divided – those Churches which have admitted women to priestly ministry have done so for serious doctrinal reasons.

In a further letter, this time addressed to Cardinal Jan Willebrands, President of the Vatican Secretariat for Promoting Christian Unity, the Archbishop wrote:

I understand that the Roman Catholic Church believes that it has
no right to change a tradition unbroken throughout the history of
the Church, universal in the East and in the West, and considered
to be truly Apostolic.

On the Anglican side there has been a growing conviction that
there exists in Scripture and Tradition no fundamental objections to
the ordination of women to the ministerial priesthood. This has
been expressed synodically by a number of provinces within the
internal debate upon this matter – a debate which has developed
with growing intensity for over forty years – Anglicans would
generally doubt whether the New Testament by itself alone permits
a clear settlement of the issue once and for all.

He goes on to say that the exclusion of women from priestly
ministry cannot be proved to be of 'divine law', but that with such
an important issue it is not enough to push ahead simply because
there are no reasons against:

It is also necessary to demonstrate compelling doctrinal reasons *for*
such a development . . . Because the humanity of Christ our High
Priest includes male and female, it is thus urged that the ministerial
priesthood should now be opened to women in order the more
perfectly to represent Christ's inclusive High Priesthood.

This argument makes no judgement upon the past, but is
strengthened today by the fact that the representational nature of
the ministerial priesthood is actually weakened by a solely male
priesthood, when exclusively male leadership has been largely
surrendered in many human societies.

Throughout this correspondence, the Archbishop cites all the
arguments as those put forward by various factions within the
Anglican Communion rather than his own personal views, in keeping, of course, with Synodical governance; however, he consistently
refers to the arguments in favour, not those against, adding reports
to the effect that where women have been ordained the experience
has been generally beneficial. All that he does say with regard to his
own feelings – and herein lies the crunch – is that he is not
convinced that the Anglicans should go it alone, however positive
the arguments, until there is a wider consensus in both Churches.
Towards the end of what is a lengthy letter to Cardinal Willebrands,

he again makes it clear that unity is paramount: 'When sister Churches have been estranged for 400 years, but at last begin to see tangible signs of reconciliation, it is particularly painful to find this new obstacle between us.' That the Archbishop writes of women's ordination being an obstacle to unity rather than the other way around demonstrates clearly which he considers to be the more important issue.

In his reply, the Cardinal showed no sign of compromise:

> The ordination only of men to the presbyterate and episcopate is the unbroken Tradition of the Catholic and Orthodox Churches. Neither Church understands itself to be competent to alter this Tradition. In 1976, the Congregation for the Doctrine of the Faith, in the declaration *Inter Insigniores*, stated clearly that 'the Catholic Church does not consider herself to be authorised to admit women to priestly ordination'. The principal reason put forward in the declaration was that of Tradition. The constant Tradition of the Catholic and Orthodox Churches has considered the practice of Christ and the Apostles as a norm from which she could not deviate. The practice of the Church to ordain only men embodies her fidelity under the guidance of the Holy Spirit to what was given by Christ.

He continues with a warning:

> The Catholic Church takes very seriously the considerable progress that has been made towards our eventual goal of full communion of faith and sacramental life. Our greater unity must be a fundamental concern, and it has to be stated frankly that a development like the ordination of women does nothing to deepen the communion between us and weakens the communion that currently exists. The ecclesiological implications are serious.

The Cardinal's letter is dated 17 June 1986. There has been no official shift in Rome's thinking since that time.

In his letter, the Cardinal refers to those in the Anglican Communion who are opposed to the ordination of women on the grounds that so radical a departure from Tradition (always with a capital 'T') cannot be undertaken independently of Rome and the Orthodox Church. Among these opponents, John Selwyn Gummer, prominent member of the General Synod and a government minister, is, perhaps, the most outspoken – though he voted in favour of women deacons. People associated with MOW refer to him as 'the Enemy' with an 'E' as capital as the Cardinal's 'T', but he was one of the few people I interviewed who spoke without venom.

He feels that the Church of England is generally in something of a mess, with prevarication the mood of the moment rather than the firm and decisive leadership he says is needed. 'If it stood up for the faith the Church would be fuller. The full churches are those teaching an uncompromising faith. The Church of England is always out-of-date. At the moment it's stuck in the 1960s – the undisciplined sixties, while the rest of society is rediscovering discipline.'

Like so many Anglicans, John Gummer has chosen his Church for its broadness. He describes himself as an Anglo-Catholic, but says the orders of the Church are as valid for people like him as they are for the Orthodox and the evangelicals: 'This universal Church is the direct successor to the primitive Church – it is a very clear view but it holds a wide range and this broadness is its strength. It is amenable to reason. 'The problem of the ordination of women is that it assaults the nature of the Church of England and its way of determining doctrine. The Church of England has never had any distinctive doctrines. It got through the Reformation relatively unscathed and maintained the essential elements of the universal church – acceptance of the Creed, which cannot be unilaterally altered.'

His feeling is that the Church of England will draw back from ordaining women because it will not want to take such a step without universal approval, in keeping with its history of maintaining a mid-point on doctrine in order to accommodate a wide spectrum of belief. Emphasising the 'broadness' of the Church of England, John Gummer says that he, personally, believes in the Immaculate Conception but adds that this is not part of the necessary teaching of the Church. His belief and that of other Anglicans who do not believe in the virgin birth can be quite happily accommodated together, but in the matter of women priests there is a terrible impasse. General Synod moves towards admitting women to full priesthood are taking years, spent to a large extent in preparing legislation that will make it possible for those 'against' to remain within the Church. So, while nothing of the sort is needed to enable pew-sharing by those whose fundamental beliefs vary with regard to the degree of acceptance and non-acceptance of the 'Virgin' Mary, even now, some of the best brains in the country are attempting to draft legislation that will satisfy those who cannot accept women at the altar, yet somehow would have to if the day comes and they want to stay.

Whether one is 'for' or 'against', this seems incredible. Why should the one situation need this sort of legislation when both are surely fundamental in terms of tradition?

Legislation or not, John Gummer and many like him say they will not stay if women are to preside at the Eucharist. He does not believe that they have the right or the ability, and that this is all to do with the central mystery of the Church. He already eschews churches in America, where he frequently visits, if he knows there is a woman conducting the service. 'If the Church of England does allow women priests I will make alternative arrangements. I will be forced to conclude that Cardinal Newman was right, that the Church of England is not part of the Catholic Church, but a sect.'

All this said, it was difficult to sit in his ministerial office in Whitehall, hardly a stone's throw from Downing Street, without thinking of the woman incumbent there and MOW's forceful, feminist arguements for the equality that is in every other walk of life in the late twentieth century. John Gummer dismisses this line of thought as irrelevant. 'It seems to me that Our Lord chose the moment of Incarnation. He could have chosen now — today is just as much a cultural prison as two thousand years ago. The point is, we have not chosen ours, but He chose His.' There is really no arguing with this. It is the neatest wiping out of all the reasoning based on sociological and cultural considerations; in other words, if God had wanted women priests, Christ would be on earth now, in the liberated 1980s, selecting a mixed band of apostles. But, no, He chose two thousand years ago, and He chose men. This would, perhaps, explain why the Jews have, in some cases, allowed women to be rabbis: if they are still waiting for the Messiah, who is to say which sex will be adopted in the coming messianic human form?

A woman 'Christa' would certainly perplex the Roman Catholics.
Cardinal Willebrands states:

> Feminine imagery is used to reveal the place of the human family
> in God's plan of salvation. In the Old Testament, the people of
> Israel is depicted as the bride of Yahweh. In the New Testament St
> Paul speaks of the Church as the bride of Christ. In its tradition,
> the Church has understood itself in terms of this feminine imagery
> and symbolism as the Body which received the Word of God, and
> which is fruitful in virtue of that which has been received. Mary,
> the Mother of God, is, in her response to the Word of God, a type
> of the Church. Christ, on the other hand, is the Head of the Body,
> and it is through the Head that the whole Body is redeemed. It is
> precisely in this perspective that the representative role of the
> ministerial priesthood is to be understood.

John Gummer says that one of the biggest problems for him is
that he is asking other people (women) to make the sacrifices,
although he feels that the 'heresy' of the twentieth century is
believing that Christianity is not about sacrifice. 'It is the "too hard"
attitude of the liberals, trying to make the fundamental parts of the
Church less painful. In order to make good things happen there has
to be sacrifice – these things are born out of pain. An example is the
question of homosexual practice – those who, by nature, are
homosexual are constrained in the same way as those who are
heterosexual – sex is only acceptable in marriage.'

The Church's obsession with sex is shown again in the way in
which the issue of women's ordination is, repeatedly, discussed in
the same breath as the issue of homosexual clergy. It seems as if, by
instinct rather than reason, the two, very separate, problems have
been lumped together by Synod under the one heading 'deviance'.
Both are an embarrassment to the Church, but the way in which the
two have been linked seems almost mischievous, as if homosexual
practices and being a woman are equally sinful barriers to ordination.

It is surprising that those who are campaigning for women's
ordination have not made more of a fuss about the way the two
issues have been discussed together. To an outsider, the high-profile

Synod debate on homosexuals, which captured the imagination of the press with headlines like 'Pulpit poofs can stay' and 'Synod clash looms over debate on sex', seemed almost like a subconscious attempt to divert public attention from the issue of women priests and at the same time debase and trivialise it by linking the two. For the purpose of writing this book I subscribed to a press cuttings service, requesting all reports referring to women priests. During the last months of 1987 and the first of 1988 I received countless cuttings in which the main subject was homosexuals in the Church, but somewhere down the text there would be a reference to women priests. In a major article in the *Independent* on 20 January 1988, the Archbishop of Canterbury talked to journalist Andrew Brown about the previous "testing year". In the introductory paragraph, Brown stated: 'The General Synod voted in February [1987] to prepare legislation for the ordination of women to the priesthood; in November, it passed a resolution condemning homosexual behaviour, which was vociferously criticised as a fudge.' In fact both resolutions were something of a 'fudge', as firm and final decisions were not made about either issue. What is noteworthy is that, in four columns of text, nearly half is devoted to homosexual clergy but only three lines to women priests.

As far as unity with Rome is concerned, sexual practices would appear to be as divisive an issue as that of women priests, and yet there does not seem to have been much, if any, consideration given by Synod to this point. The greater cause of unity has been cited over and over again as the major reason for the Church of England to hold back over its decision on women priests, but how does Rome react to 'Pulpit poofs can stay' – Rome with its stern morals and celibacy?

There can be no doubt that the present movement in the Church of England towards women's full ordination has knocked back progress with the Catholics, while American action in electing a woman to the episcopate is described as 'the major problem' for worldwide Anglican accord with Rome. Nevertheless, ARCIC II, the second Anglican/Roman Catholic International Commission, charged with the task of studying the ordination of women, has declared itself determined to pursue the quest for eventual unity.

One intriguing possibility is that in theory Rome could get there first in ordaining women to the priesthood. In the Church of England it is the democratic process that is holding up progress, but the Pope could make a decision overnight. Even more interesting is the question: if he did, would the Anglicans immediately follow suit? Either way, the Anglicans would be in a sticky position: continued debate and delay would indicate sexism to have been at the root of the issue all along, while instant capitulation would suggest adherence to papal supremacy.

The Chairman of the Church of England's Board of Mission and Unity for the past six years feels that Rome could get there first. Recently retired from the post, Daphne Wales is the only woman to have chaired one of the Church's four main Boards. Her impression, gained at the highest level in dealing with matters of unity, is that Rome is already shifting its position, most notably by including women in its official delegations.

Miss Wales, for thirteen years a member of the General Synod, is in favour of women priests, but, like many prominent members of her Church, does not see the issue as paramount. 'The biggest task is the mission of the Church,' she says. 'The ordination of women is an intrinsic part and I am perfecty sure it will come, but I am not prepared to say when. 'The legislation is very difficult, the nitty-gritty very controversial. Synod has accepted that there are some priests who for conscientious reasons would not want to work with women.'

Daphne Wales, although reluctant to predict when it will happen, believes that without a masterstroke from Rome, it may take more than another five years for the House of Clergy to alter its position.

Another Synod member, more of a 'backbencher' compared with Miss Wales's former 'ministerial' position, is Clive Cresswell, who has been in the House of Laity for the past five years. A supporter of women's ordination, he too sees a weakening in the unity issue as a barrier to women's progress. 'It's certainly an argument that will continue to be made, but it's not so strong now as, say, five years ago. The laity is very much aware of a strong undercurrent in the Roman Catholic Church in favour of women priests.'

Like Miss Wales, Clive Cresswell thinks the final draft legislation to allow women priests in the Church of England will be defeated in the House of Clergy. 'The crunch year is 1992, and if defeated it will not come up again for a long time. With the elections for the new Synod coming up in 1990 I know already of [Anglican] Catholics who are making sure they will return 'traditionalist' candidates.'

He does not think the Church will fall apart if women are kept out of the priesthood for what would be an unforeseeable number of years. 'My personal opinion, which is shared by many others, is that this would be the testing time, and I think the discipline in the Church of England is such that people will not break away. Some may go into the Nonconformist Churches, but the number will be few.'

Support for the ordination of women was one of Clive Cresswell's 'platforms' for election to Synod and he is still keen to see it happen, but he describes the present mood in Synod as one of ennui. 'People are fed up with the issue and think far too much importance is attached to it. Synod has taken the step of asking for legislation to be drawn up and we've just got to wait now. There are other matters in the Church of England besides the ordination of women,' he said, adding that, as he spoke, there were only sixty-six women training for ordination in England.

Synodical government of the Church has been in practice for less than twenty years, and a review of how it is working will be completed in the next few years. Whether or not the insufficient majority in favour of seeing those sixty-six women (and those who preceded and follow them) ordained to the full priesthood will use this review as an opportunity to alter the Synodical rules to further their purpose seems unlikely.

'It's very difficult to explain how people who have faith think about these things and make decisions,' says Clive Cresswell. 'When you go into the hierachy of the Church of England, sometimes you despair.' I was listening to him a couple of days after the February 1989 Synod, when moves to create positive discrimination to increase the number of black members in the House of Laity had been defeated.

Was this another instance of the Church of England dodging the issue? If positive discrimination is to be viewed as progress, then the democratic workings of Synod appear to be getting in the way. A decision from Rome to ordain women might expose a quiet reactionary core within Synod that has hitherto voted in favour of the principle of women's ordination in the belief that it will never happen. It is highly unlikely that the present Pope would make such a decision, but it is not impossible that an American Pope could be in the Vatican before long; and American Anglicans have been ordaining women for more than a decade.

SEVEN

Anglicans abroad

The tortuous debate that continues in the Church of England over the ordination of women is similarly being enacted in almost every other Anglican corner of the world. There are now well over a thousand women priests in the Anglican Communion in many different countries, including Brazil, Canada, Hong Kong, Kenya, New Zealand, Polynesia, Puerto Rico, Uganda and the USA; and women deacons in Cuba, Ireland, Japan, Scotland, South Africa and Wales. In other provinces resistance is growing: in Papua New Guinea, for example, the only province where every bishop has signed a declaration against the ordination of women, there are moves to join forces with Rome. Even where women are now ordained to the priesthood the agony is not over. The feared 'schism', if not already a reality in England, is happening elsewhere: in America where women are priests but many of those who opposed the move still find themselves unable to accept a woman at the altar; in Australia, where women are further away from attaining ordination than they are in England, and activists are now turning from the Church, sacrificing the Eucharist and even contemplating hunger strikes. I visited both these countries, as they are representative of the situation 'before' and 'after'.

To understand the Australian situation the country has to be seen as a divided nation. Politically the different states have a considerable degree of autonomy and the same applies to the Church and its

95

diocesan synods. As long ago as 1976 the Melbourne Synod passed the principle of ordination, but the Sydney Diocese, the largest in Australia, remains firmly opposed and to date holds sway – but only just.

The matter came to a head at the end of 1987 when a Special General Synod was called solely to try and resolve the ordination issue. The previous year a number of dioceses had begun to ordain women to the diaconate but some, like Sydney, were still holding back.

During 1985 and 1986 the Australian MOW, led by the charismatic Dr Patricia Brennan, who hosts her own national TV programme, mounted a high-profile campaign which succeeded in bringing the issue to the attention of the general public and generated intense media interest. As a result, a television film was made, documenting the run-up to the Special Synod, and the cameras were there on the day to record what was expected to be the moment of victory. In the event, the scene captured on film was one of defeat. Just two votes kept the women out. 'MOW members, women and men, sitting in the visitors' gallery, were stunned, then appalled, and made a prophetic announcement that women would seek to pursue their calling outside the Church until such time as the Church repented.' MOW's own report of the proceedings continues: 'Those women and men then left the gallery weeping and singing whilst the Synod members sat in silence. Many of those members joined MOW outside and wept with us. Members of the press were in tears. The national media broadcast the shame of a Church unable to abandon its sexism.'

In the official report of the Sydney Diocesan Commission on the Ordination of Women the beliefs that led to the Special Synod decision are summed up in the following paragraph:

Insofar as within this debate there is discussion concerning the nature of God and its disclosure in scriptural language, we would affirm that scriptural language about God is inspired by God, and we are not at liberty to modify or change it. While it is patent that God, being God, is neither man nor woman, he reveals himself in masculine terms. This is no denigration of femaleness but remains essential to a Christian understanding of God, and is an aspect of God's self-disclosure, which lies outside human authority to change.

Despite such a pronouncement, since the 1987 Special Synod, Australian bishops have tried to soften the blow and in February 1988 issued a press release in an attempt to resolve tension within the Church between the two factions. Their statement calls for overall unity whether or not women are eventually ordained, as legally they could be in individual dioceses, despite the theological objection expressed by Sydney. But for the militants of MOW this does not go far enough. They hear talk of unity as hypocrisy, and demonstrated their feelings with a protest demonstration in Perth when the Archbishop of Canterbury visited in February 1988 and preached to 8,000 people at the city's entertainments centre. There were only about twenty demonstrators, but the world's press reported the banner-waving and not the sermon.

The guerrilla camp on the edge of the Church

'Sydney is one of the toughest places in the world for women, but starting MOW was like picking up a relay baton – as soon as I had it everyone else wanted it,' Patricia Brennan told me when we talked at the Sydney Hilton.

A few minutes before this she had met me off a plane from Melbourne. 'Mel*bun*, not Mel*bourne* – that's something we correct with you Brits,' she had said. MOW in the UK has got the accent wrong as well, not prophetic enough, according to Dr Brennan: 'The Movement for the Ordination of Women is about prophecy,' she says. 'We are going for a prophetic ministry. Our methods are confrontational, whereas I believe British MOW is working hand-in-glove with the Church. In Australia MOW is like a guerrilla camp on the edge of the Church.'

Patricia Brennan has been an Anglican all her life. She worked in Africa as a medical missionary, sent there by the Missionary Society. She has little to say that is good about her Church, but is unequivocal in expressing absolute love for it. She got MOW going in Australia in

1983 and is now the national president. She started the movement
in her own diocese, Sydney, and took it nationwide in 1984 with
the help of UK MOW leader Monica Furlong, who came over to give
the new movement international standing with a public-speaking
tour which covered the country.

As we spoke, Patricia Brennan kept emphasising this idea of
prophecy — of herself as a prophet: 'A prophet has to be self-
declared,' she says, 'and I've weathered the terrible stuff of self-
doubt, although it's an uphill battle every day and I know I'm seen
as a strident banshee. I think I'm regarded as less spiritual than
people would like, autocratic, irreverent. I've always been slightly
uncomfortable in the conservatism of Anglicanism. I have a terrible
lack of ease with any system that crunches people under it. I don't
draw my strength from the Church, I draw it from people.

'I have no megalomaniacal notion of myself, and increasingly it
matters less to me personally about being a priest. MOW has helped
women escape. There are no rules that say you can't 'stay alive' just
because you're not in the Church.'

Despite her 'guerrilla camp' position, singularly symbolised by
her decision not to receive the Eucharist again until women are
ordained priests, Dr Brennan says she is still in favour of unity. Her
point is that the Eucharist itself is no longer a mark of true unity but
of disunity. She believes that the ordination of women is the final
frontier, and until this equality is achieved there will be domestic
violence in the House of God.

The 'domestic violence' referred to by Patricia Brennan is not the
real thing cited by the Rev. Chris Albany as symptomatic of a
dangerously extreme patriarchal society. Chris Albany is a member
of MOW, and he believes that to open up the feminine in the Church
will make it more 'whole' and perhaps lead the way in a country
where a recent survey revealed that 25 per cent of Australians feel
that domestic violence is OK.

'Husbands beating wives is the end result of a patriarchal society,'
he explained at his home in Perth. 'This is at least what is at issue —
a repressive society which does not allow men or women to be

themselves. Masculine attributes are particularly held up in Australia, and the feminine downgraded.'

The truth of this is, perhaps, demonstrated in the title of the television documentary mentioned earlier in this chapter *The Fully-Ordained Meat Pie*. These words come from an interview with Australian Anglican traditionalist, Father Ian Herring, who told the documentary-makers that ordaining a woman would be not much different from ordaining a meat pie.

Father Herring and other clergy who express their opposition to women's ordination in such extreme and emotive terms were given the 'anti' platform in the film. The result was a display of buffoonery which somehow succeeded in downgrading the case for women. Chris Albany feels the film would have been more powerful if more reasoned argument from the 'anti' camp had been used. His wife, Pam, who organised the Perth demonstration during Dr Runcie's visit, did not see this point, but her desire for women to be acknowledged in the Church is so intense that she perhaps sees all opposition as inane. Her own words are fierce: 'The bottom line for most clergy is in their hip pocket, keeping their job and not bucking the bishop. We demonstrated when Runcie came because the Perth service was meant to be a display of unity and that was hypocrisy. It's just not the case that the Church is unified.

'Most people ignored us as they went into the service but Patricia [Brennan] called out to Runcie, 'Pray for us,' and he said he would. All the TV coverage focused on the demonstration and not the Eucharist. The diocesan media officer was really caught with his pants down!'

Chris Albany was in the unusual position of being part of both the service and the demonstration, and, careless of his 'hip pocket', told the television cameras that his bishop did not have the courage to go ahead and ordain women. The Archbishop of Perth has declared himself in favour, but like his colleagues who share this view, will not go against the majority decision.

Australian MOW has nothing like the membership of that in the UK, a couple of hundred at most, but the leaders are vociferous and their methods are reminiscent of the suffragettes. Patricia Brennan admits that fasting to the point of sickness is something she has discussed with her fellow members and remains a consideration. Long ago the MOW activists realised that they would not be able to fight for ordination from within Synod, and they now openly accuse dioceses such as Sydney of gerrymandering in Synod selection.

'We thought we were going to win at the Special Synod,' says Dr Brennan, 'but it was a hideous defeat and caused unexpected heartbreak.'

In a subsequent paper published by MOW, the conclusion is:

> The bishops have agreed to wait upon the 1989 General Synod decision. This is in the face of Sydney's continued opposition, which may well mean the vote is lost again.
>
> In despair women are leaving the Church, though there are many who are just emerging from their fear of facing the issue and are joining MOW. Not only are Anglican women looking for decisive action, but Catholic women and men are seeing MOW as an agent of change for their situation. Catholic women are working with Anglicans to see women ordained so that the Catholic Church will be similarly challenged.

Not one of the MOW women I spoke to in Australia had any personal desire to attain priesthood, not any more. It seems that the 'cause' has become far more important than individual vocation. 'We're always right on the edge of slipping out of the Church – it's so draining,' said Eileen Diesendorf, prominent in MOW and author of a thesis on why women are leaving the Church. A recent survey in Australia showed a significant number of professional women leaving because they could not accept being second-class citizens within their Church, when they were no longer so at work.

Many of the women Eileen Diesendorf interviewed said that, for them, the Church had become an oppressive institution, while it was claiming to be helping them to be free. 'The realisation that this was the case was a long time coming. Each of the women struggled in her own situation to be what the Church said she should be. For some time, each believed it was her fault she was not succeeding. . . . The irony is that these women left because they were attempting to find deeper spirituality or to become more committed and involved.'

The 'anti' lobby takes a quite different view on why the Church is losing its flock, citing lack of authority, 'decay flowing from modernist and revisionist acceptance of secular pressures.' These last words come from Michael Barnard's article in the *Church Chronicle* in September 1987, a month after the Special Synod had said 'no' to women.

> These pressures are best illustrated in England by the closure over three decades of 2000 of the nation's 16,000 churches and a drop in regular worship to a mere 3 per cent; and in Australia, where the Anglican is again by far the largest nominal religious group, a drop in regular church attendance to at best 14 per cent [of the population] and almost certainly much lower.

Michael Barnard's vitriolic article begins: 'If a postscript were needed to the Anglican Synod's rejection of women's ordination to the priesthood, it would surely rest on the peculiar response of the losers. This, to say the least, has been less than gracious.' He continues further on:

> The 'weeping and gnashing of teeth' by women demonstrators outside St Andrew's Cathedral chapter house and the tendency of frustrated MOW lobbyists to scatterblast those of unlike mind with epithets such as 'chauvinistic', 'sexist' and 'blatantly discriminatory' place an important question mark over the temperamental suitability of some women to face the pressures of priesthood. Many demands are placed on priests, not least of which is to cope gracefully with adversity and in so doing to set an example for others. . . .
> 'Women,' Dr Brennan is quoted, 'are used to being devastated in the Church.' If, indeed, the resistance to women priests is to be seen in such apocalyptic terms, what words are left adequately to describe the emerging situation in England where, if present policies prevail, a clergyman opposed to women priests will be barred from consecration as a bishop, yet one who disputes or denies the Divinity of Christ, the Virgin Birth or the Resurrection will face no such automatic impediment? Sexual 'equality' is truly a remarkable thing.

The United States

At the end of September 1988 I was in the United States when the Episcopal Church elected its first woman bishop and I was asked why women had been ordained for more than a decade over there and not in England. The person who asked the question had no connection with the Church, which was probably why she could make such a straightforward enquiry about a subject so taxing and convoluted that it continues to split American Anglicans twelve years on.

My answer to her was, nonetheless, quite simple. American women forced the hand of their Church by being loud and militant in their demand for ordination, and taking 'illegal' action which could not be ignored. Perhaps if women in England had taken the same hard-line approach they too would have achieved their goal, during that surge in the climate of feminism which was the 1970s.

The drive for the ordination of women to the priesthood began in earnest in 1970 when the Episcopal Church decided to ordain women to the diaconate. Early attempts to extend this to the priesthood were defeated, but on 29 July 1974 eleven women in Philadelphia were 'illegally' ordained to the full priesthood by three retired bishops. Less than three years later (from 1 January 1977) women were being legally ordained and, to add to the controversy, some were openly lesbian, leading many people to connect women's ordination with moral decline. The issue of sexual orientation aside, bishops who had voted for women priests soon discovered that they had problems with the male clergy in their dioceses who were theologically opposed to the move. One bishop is reported to have said: 'It is like trying to minister to a man when you have just run over his child.'

Schism was a reality, manifest at its most ugly by lawsuits for the possession of church property where congregations split in two. The number of Episcopalians who transferred to dissident churches is now estimated at around 15,000, said to be only half of 1 per cent of all Episcopalians; but the more damaging figure is shown in the decline in Church membership over the past decade, from 2.5

million to 1.7, although there is some confusion as the method of counting has altered during this period. In fact it is claimed that church attendance has increased by 28 per cent since the ordination of women, although at the same time, the Episcopalians express concern at the drop in membership.

Today, there are over a thousand women priests in America, but in general women are still finding it difficult to become leaders in the church. The Rev. Linda Grenz, at the Office of Women in Mission and Ministry of the Episcopal Church, says: 'In twelve years we have come a long way and not very far at all. It is fairly easy now to get the first job out of seminary – people see it as a nice balance to have a woman curate and a male rector. The next slot is harder to find. We have an over-supply of clergy.

'It is a matter of tradition that leadership is male. Sexism is alive and well in the Church. Most of the up-front prejudice against women priests is from women; the 'system' has made women compete with one another. The ordination of women does not change oppression – it is not a panacea.'

Linda says that getting the job interview is the important step for women because in most cases they are better qualified and more gifted than the male candidates: 'If you are not better than the men, you simply don't get through the system.'

The underlying concern in many parishes is that men will leave if a woman is appointed incumbent, that her leadership will not be accepted. 'My concern,' says Linda Grenz, 'is that the Church will be left to women, and men will go on with running the society that dominates women. No one in this church is looking at how to "engage" men.'

This, no doubt, includes Linda Grenz's own movement, committed to the full participation of women in the Church. It has been suggested that all congregations should be assigned a woman as an interim priest when a parish has a vacancy, this being considered the best way to change the minds of those who are against women clergy. The idea was published in a recent report by the Committee for the Full Participation of Women in the Church. It was also noted that fear of reverse discrimination disinclines men to support such measures. The general feeling seems to be that there is widespread support for equal opportunity but significant resistance to affirmative action.

'It is sometimes the case that activities in which many women engage are not perceived as important or powerful enough to be of interest to men,' the Committee reports, referring to the fear that men will be driven away from the church by women in the pulpit and in lay leadership. 'But such fears seem to undervalue men's faithfulness and commitment and the actual facts suggest that men may become more active when women share in leadership responsibilities.'

'Actual facts' are quite difficult to root out. According to a recent Gallup poll (as reported in a WAOW 'pull-out' from the English *Church Times*) 49 per cent of Episcopalians are opposed to women in the priesthood. I put this to Nell Gibson, executive assistant to the Bishop of New York, who said the figure was more like 15 to 20 per cent. 'There has been a really beautiful acceptance, very open and loving,' she said, 'even by people who were against.'

It is undeniable that there are still many Episcopalians who have not been able to accept women priests, but they have remained within the official Church, the one that is part of the worldwide Anglican Communion and whose bishops are invited to the Lambeth Conference. Those who could neither accept nor remain have formed themselves into a series of 'continuing' churches, and not one of their bishops was to be seen at Lambeth in 1988. However, numbered among the officially accredited Press Corps was Mrs Auburn Faber Traycik, eiditor of the *Christian Challenge* and a primary spokesperson for the Continuing Church.

Auburn Traycik, a smart and handsome woman who looks rather like a young version of the romantic novelist Barbara Cartland, has recently moved her 'operation' from Austin, Texas, to Washington DC. She wanted a more prominent position for the office of her magazine, which reaches twenty-five countries but only 5,000 subscribers. In both Austin and Washington she has initiated new congregations for the Continuing Church. Born and raised an Episcopalian, she 'came out' in 1978, no longer feeling at home in the Church she had loved.

The hard-hitting magazine she edits was started in 1961 by her mother, Dorothy Faber, who remained editor until her death in 1982. Auburn's husband Louis, a former lawyer and public prosecutor turned seminarian, took over until 1986, when he began full-time study for ordination.

'Over the years, tumultuous changes in the Church have been noted in the *Challenge*. It is a watchdog magazine and not appreciated,' Mrs Traycik says. 'Sex runs through all the controversies. This is where all the tumult is, in the gender issues. I agree with the Bishop of London: we are talking about the created order for men and women in the world and a movement against this on all fronts. All the issues of gender are on the line — homosexuality, inclusive language. There are extremists who are taking the Episcopal Church to a Goddess religion with a lot of male-repudiation and woman-worship.'

Mrs Traycik says that 500 Episcopal Churches have closed in the past decade, yet few, if any, have been taken over by the Continuing Churches, of which there are seven main jurisdictions and about 400 congregations; they are buying or building their own places for worship, consecrated by the men they have made their bishops.

Auburn Traycik, despite the warring tone of her magazine and its 'tabloid-like' inclination for stories about self-confessed lesbian deacons and transsexual nuns, describes what has happened in America as a genteel schism. She blames the Episcopal Church for failing to encourage women in their more proper ministries, which, if it had done so, might have negated the movement for women priests: 'Men need the priesthood more than women,' she says. 'Women are already good and caring.'

I asked her how she saw the future panning out and she talked of the doctrine of reception, a testing period to discover the Will of God: 'Women deacons in the early Church were no longer considered valid after a time and then no longer ordained. My best guess is that interest could be lost and the ordination of women may decline, but I don't know how the women priests left would be catered for.' More immediately, she envisages the strengthening of the Continuing Churches through the likely creation of a loose association that will link them into provinces (groups of dioceses with an archbishop at their head) in a similar fashion to that of the recognised Anglican Communion. Nevertheless, she still thinks her bishops should be invited to the next Lambeth Conference.

Obviously, she was disappointed by the inconclusive outcome of Lambeth '88, but then so were Linda Grenz and her colleagues, who felt that the bishops were dealing with the 'problem' of women rather than supporting them. Equally dissatisfied was the Rt Rev. Robert Mercer, the former Anglican Bishop of Matabeleland who has now accepted an appointment as assistant bishop of the Continuing Church in Canada (where women have been ordained for years). In Auburn Traycik's *Christian Challenge*, he is reported as saying: 'Liberalism can only die, because it's got nothing for which to live. What unites them? Property and finance, nothing else. It's not faith. It's not doctrine.'

Referring to the decisions taken at Lambeth, he told me: 'We used to have good dialogue with the RCs in Matabeleland, but the folly of Lambeth is likely to terminate that. Affluent middle-class Americans are not necessarily very interested in rapprochement with Rome. But in drought-stricken, poverty-stricken, terrorist-ridden Matabeleland, unity with the largest, most committed and most able of the other missionary denominations is simply a necessity. In fortifying the wall between Roman Catholics and Anglicans, the Lambeth Conference has done a great disservice both to mission and to humanitarian work in Zimbabwe.'

Bishop Mercer's view, gained from first-hand experience, puts a different angle on the desirability of unity with Rome. He takes it beyond a theological ideal, shaming the intellectual debate. And there is a further dimension to be considered: how can Rome allow the advent of Anglican women priests to hamper ecumenical work in Third World countries?

Meanwhile, the American 'antis' are obsessed by the distinction between male and female, seeing one of the responsibilities of the Church to be the maintenance of this distinction. They say that the ordination of women is all to do with a desire for androgyny, the blurring of the sexes, which is why the issue of women priests is bundled up with the Church's stance on homosexuals. Those who have left the Episcopal Church during the past decade say that there were three main reasons for their departure, the ordination of women, changes to the Prayer Book, and moral decline. All three have to do with sex, even the Prayer Book, because it is the shift towards inclusive language and gradual de-sexing of God that troubles them.

The weakness of the Continuing Churches is in their division, a state of affairs they themselves describe as shameful, crippling and intolerable. The causes are said to be numerous but include clashing ambitions and personalities, and incompatible ideas of canonical law and church government. They are attempting to do something about this disunity but the way ahead is unclear.

Mainstream Episcopalians seem largely to have disregarded the Continuing Churches; in fact Nell Gibson was uncertain as to what they were and even of their existence. Far from causing disunity, she claims that after the initial 'fall-out' the ordination of women has brought a new wholeness to the Church. 'Before, it was rather like a single parent bringing up a child on their own. They might have been very good at it, but in terms of that child's sense of wholeness and completeness they were not receiving a total picture.'

As yet, even with the election of the first woman bishop and after more than a decade of women priests, it seems that the picture is still little more than a sketch. Recognising this, the far from complacent American women are still challenging the system of which they are now a part. Ann Smith, who heads the Women in Mission and Ministry team at the Episcopal Church Center in New York, advocates the withholding of church funding from development work world-wide where women are not helped. 'The Church is still supporting sexism,' she says. 'The process of challenge has to happen.'

When I met her, she and her staff were preparing for a major conference in connection with the World Council of Churches' Ecumenical Decade of Churches in Solidarity with Women (1988–1998). The theme of the conference, to be held in Mexico, was to be Justice, Peace and the Integrity of Creation, the agenda packed with talk of oppression, racism, sexism, classism.

In a way, it is a pity that all this sounds so strident and, somehow, alienating. In a letter I was shown by a member of WAOW in the UK an Episcopalian nun wrote:

> How well I remember, back in the seventies, how aggressive and
> unattractive so many of the women were who were demanding
> ordination. I used to be embarrassed for them and after the thing
> went through you'd see them striding around and talking in loud
> voices and wearing pants and clerical collars, and it was *horrid*. But
> that's fast wearing off now that they realise they don't have to
> compete with men any more. I have seen some really womanly
> women priests who commanded my respect, women whom I have
> met at various gatherings who are feminine in every way.

An African experience

The 1988 Lambeth Conference clearly demonstrated the strength and spread of Anglicanism in Africa and the Third World. African bishops seemed almost to dominate the scene, but they were as divided as the Church of England over the issue of women priests, one going so far as to proclaim the movement as the work of the devil, while others compared prejudice against women with racial discrimination.

There are African provinces where the advent of women priests looks unlikely at present, but in other parts the issue is being as hotly debated as it is in England, and some provinces have already begun to ordain women. One of these is Uganda, and at the beginning of 1987 I wrote to the Rev. Deborah Micungwe, hoping that she would be able to give me some idea of her life as a woman priest in Africa. Months went by without a reply. I thought that she had perhaps not received my letter. An architect friend was due to spend two months in Uganda on a construction project. I asked him if he could take a copy of my letter with him and post it in Uganda. When he returned to the UK he told me that the postal service was erratic in some areas, but that he had given my letter to a small group of nuns travelling out to the area where the Rev. Micungwe was thought to be working. I don't know who these nuns were, but

I would like to thank them. Here is Deborah Micungwe's reply:

> My mother was a Sunday School teacher and one day she asked
> me to take her place. From that day an interest began in my heart.
> My mother told me there were Roman Catholic sisters who worked
> in the Church all their lives, and that increased my interest; but in
> our Anglican church no girls or women worked in the Church at
> that time, and I wished I could be a Catholic so that I could join a
> sisterhood.
>
> As the years went by, two of my school mates joined a
> theological training college because the chance was extended to
> girls who wished to work in the Church as commissioned workers.
> This thrilled me very much, yet although women could work in the
> Church, they could not be ordained.
>
> When I got saved (i.e., I gave my life to Christ) that gave me an
> opportunity to go to different churches in our village and outside
> to give my testimony of how Jesus saved me. The saved brethren
> put me in their preaching teams. I preached the gospel every time
> there was a mission, conference or other Church outreach.
>
> One evening when I was going for a fellowship meeting with
> brethren, a thought struck me: Deborah, why can't you go to study
> for a diploma in theology? After the meeting I shared this with a
> brother in Christ who introduced me to a student at the theological
> training college. He told me the procedure to follow, which included
> a written and an oral interview. I passed and was admitted into
> Bishop Tucker Theological College, where I found other girls, eleven
> of them.
>
> During my time at College the training was the same for women
> as for men. On graduation day both were issued with certificates to
> certify that he or she had completed an ordination course.
>
> What was painful to me was the practical side of training, to
> learn things which as a woman I would never be able to put into
> practice, e.g., conducting Holy Communion, baptism and marriage
> services. As each of the male ordinands was asked to preside at
> Holy Communion I almost shed tears, because I felt that as a
> woman I would never be made a priest.
>
> Some dioceses were ordaining women to be deacons, but my
> diocese of Kigezi was not doing so. I looked for ways and means
> how to move from my diocese to another where I could be made a
> deacon, but I failed. A commissioned woman worker would always
> be headed by a male priest, who was often academically lower than
> she was herself; or maybe both priest and commissioned woman
> held the same qualification, yet the man was always the head. One

other point was the fact that our uniforms as commissioned workers
often caused people to mistake us for nurses!

When I completed my four-year training, I was commissioned as
a Church worker (similar to a lay reader). I was posted as an
assistant pastor to work with a priest. He had the same qualifications
as me, but he was three years ahead of me in the College.

On the day I arrived nobody was there to meet me, which
was unusual in my diocese because a lay reader or a pastor is
always welcomed by the Christians. The reason this church
refused to welcome me was that the vicar requested an assistant
pastor from the Bishop, and the Christians did not like the idea
at all. Some thought I was the Pastor's girlfriend and that was
why he had sent for me. It was a shock to learn that Christians
did not want me to work among them. But this dislike gradually
faded away and by the end of five years they all liked me, and
many times I was asked to be Godmother to their children, and
later, when I was transferred, the majority gave parties in my
honour, and some accompanied me to the new church, and
continued to visit and encourage me.

During one four-month period I was left in charge of the parish
(while the vicar went away for further studies) and all the Christians
supported me in my work. Sunday collections increased, and money
for building materials was donated to put up my house. No
accommodation had been prepared for me when I arrived, and I
needed to be near the church to open it early each morning and
close it late in the evening, so I stayed with the vicar. It was most
difficult during the war of 1979 when he moved his family away.
Three times I met soldiers who asked me questions. One day a
soldier said: 'This man loves you,' and I replied: 'Oh thank you for
that love, thank you for coming to liberate Uganda, God will bless
you for that, in fact He has already blessed you.' When he realised
I was telling them about God, they left me alone.

Even though I was left in charge of the parish, the vicar would
not allow me to do some things I should have done as his assistant.
He left the chief church warden to chair a Parish Council; however,
it did not take place as, for some unknown reason, the members
did not turn up.

When I was ordained a deacon he still refused to let me baptise
children, baptising them all himself, and whenever there was a
couple to marry he would invite another male priest to do it,
although I was there to assist him, and male deacons do everything
in a parish, including baptisms and weddings. That annoyed me,

although I did teach candidates for baptism and confirmation, conducted some Sunday services, and assisted at Holy Communion by giving the cup.

I worked with three vicars and each treated me differently. I learned to be patient and tolerant, and after five years my bishop, the late Rt Rev. Dr Festo Kivengere, priested me with another two women. He gave me my own parish, Rusikizi, twenty-five miles from Kabale town. When the Christians heard I was to be priested they were so happy. The parish organised a party. The Mothers' Union wore their uniforms during the ordination service and they too organised a party.

I was in charge of this parish for three years. There were about 700 Christians, and I went there fearing they would not accept me, but I was encouraged by the way they welcomed me on the day of arrival. At the junction to the church there was a big gathering, and I found them dancing, singing, clapping hands and jumping with joy to meet me!

They walked with me to the church, where I found another big group, and I went straight into the church, which was full of people. All the seats were taken and people were standing outside. They stayed there, dancing and singing until evening time, and the first Sunday 170 people came for Communion. During the following week they brought me food, and during the three years I stayed with them, the Mothers' Union, the Youth Group and the Christian women continued to bring me gifts, and sometimes they would volunteer to work in my gardens.

I had sixteen church wardens, two lay readers, and a treasurer. They all co-operated and worked hard with me to promote our parish. In the time I was there many people were baptised and confirmed, a semi-permanent church was built, and a parish house. We made the bricks and fired them, and used iron sheets for roofing. We made a protected spring helped by an expert from England dealing with water projects in the diocese of Kigezi, and some of my friends gave me clothes and medicines so that I could provide some first aid, dressing wounds and giving out tablets for fever and worms. Poor people and school children were given the clothes.

Social problems were dealt with, for instance, on one occasion, during the Liberation War, I had to face the army officers who had been invited to settle a rape case in the parish. I had to defend the accused, who was mentally ill. Another time, a woman was caught committing adultery by her husband and when she was brought to me I settled the case and the man and his wife went happily home.

On another occasion I was accused on eight points by one man, who reported me to the Archdeacon, but the accusations were because I had refused to hand him church money and he was annoyed. At the meeting where he accused me God gave me a calmness of heart, I did not lose my temper and later we were able to put things right.

In this parish I had a weekly programme of church work; attending Fellowship meetings; counselling; teaching young people, the Mothers' Union and other women; taking funerals; visiting; preaching; baptising; and giving Holy Communion.

It was harder than ever to leave the parish when I was transferred to be chaplain in a secondary school, and I got married. The parishioners gave me many different gifts, and even now they still come to visit me. What love! I praise God for those wonderful Christians who enabled me to do the work of God.

So my views about a woman priest are:
1. She should be called to join the ministry
2. She should be trained
3. She should be courageous
4. She should be above reproach
5. She should be full of the Holy Spirit
6. She should be approachable
7. She should be willing to adjust herself according to what the ministry requires
8. She should be one who has a pastoral heart
9. She should not be easy-going!

EIGHT

Other denominations and faiths

In this chapter, six women from different faiths and denominations talk about the position and treatment of their sex in their own Churches. Their cultural backgrounds vary widely, as does their religion, yet even where equality is fundamental to doctrine, socialisation has changed this.

The women representing Islam and Sikhism clearly reveal this, but their interpretation of equality with men puts emphasis on the different roles of the sexes and displays a dignified disdain towards Western feminist militancy.

The Free Churches, who consider themselves ahead of the field in promoting women, are represented here by the Baptists. They, like the Methodists, United Reformed Church, and other Non-conformists, claim to have had less of a problem than the Anglicans because priesthood has never been at issue. They believe that Jesus was the last priest and his sacrifice beyond repetition; therefore, Nonconformist ministers are not ordained priests. Undoubtedly, this lesser clerical position has made it easier for women to enter ministry in the Free Churches, but even after nearly a century of ministerial equality there is still prejudice.

For the Jews, like the Christians, the issue is schismatic. Traditionalist Jews will have no truck with women rabbis, but the more liberal have allowed a unisex rabbinate.

Rome and the Orthodox Churches have yet to experience the

sort of struggle that is going on within Anglicanism, but the beginnings are there and the role of women in these Churches is now an issue for international debate.

The Roman Catholics

If the various denominations within Christianity were to be categor- ised into a sort of class structure, Rome would probably be seen as the aristocracy, Anglicans the great middle class, and the Free Churches somewhere in the lower order.

With this analogy in mind, it is easier to understand why Rome appears to have the upper hand in the moves towards unity, why compromise seems to be something expected of the Anglicans alone, and why the Free Churches don't really count. Unity with Rome is continually cited as the major reason why the Church of England holds back on ordaining women, while such a move would seem to be a prerequisite for any unifying action with the leading Nonconformists, who long ago admitted women to their ministries, whether or not they be called priests.

Catholic opposition to women's ordination has already been spelled out in Chapter Six. Basically, the Roman Catholic Church is not a democratic organisation like the Anglican Communion; the Pope says women can't be priests and that's all there is to it. Except for the fact that the Catholics, like the Anglicans, have a growing number of women (and men) who are finding it increasingly difficult to accept the situation. Equally, it is undeniable that for the Catholic Church the introduction of women priests would shatter the basic tenets inherent in its ritual and symbolism. This is made clear in Rome's 1976 declaration, *Inter Insigniores*, on the subject of women's ordination. Sexual symbolism, particularly that of the relationship of bridegroom to bride seen as analogous to that of Christ to the Church, is said to be integral to the way Christians from the earliest times have understood the nature of Church and sacraments, and to alter the visible terms of so fundamental a symbol as the male priest representing the male Christ is to tamper with human psychological reactions at a dangerously deep level. Countering this, it has been argued that such symbolism, if followed consistently, would mean that only women should represent the Church. Joan Morris, in her book *The Lady was a Bishop*, states:

> The fact that women were not ordained to the consecration of the Eucharist is a tradition of long standing, but based on a quite erroneous scientific understanding of genetics. It would be ridiculous to continue a tradition based on such a fallacy. To maintain that only men can represent Christ in the act of sacrifice is carrying an analogy too far. If only men can represent Christ, then only women can represent the Church — the spouse of Christ. But in baptism there is no discrimination of the sexes.

Joan Morris has long been a member of the St Joan's International Alliance, the only official Roman Catholic organisation that devotes itself to the advancement of women. St Joan's is recognised at the United Nations, is active on issues like slavery and female genital mutilation, and has been in existence most of this century. It is said to be running out of steam, but other para-Church organisations are taking over. There are radical groups like the Roman Catholic Feminists, and the more mainstream Catholic Women's Network which was founded in 1984.

Prominent in the Network and a founder-member, Alexina Murphy is a Catholic who works with the Anglican MOW, marvels at their seeming patience and expresses a radical, feminist view unexpected in so quietly spoken a mother of four, living in Roehampton.

'Perhaps it's because what they want is within reach,' she says, answering her own question: how can MOW be so patient? 'It's not such a large carrot for good behaviour in the Catholic Church — it won't happen in our lifetime.'

Good behaviour? Is this how a Catholic feminist sees the way to ordination?

'No, not really. Justice is the issue, and unity between the Churches achieved in spite of women's ordination would not be a true unity.'

Alexina Murphy has been a Catholic all her life and like all her RC contemporaries, grew up believing that she belonged to the One

True Church. Indeed, I remember as a child being told by my dearest friend, a Catholic, that I would not go to heaven because I was not of the true faith.

For Alexina this exclusive Catholic conviction was one of two major pieces of childhood conditioning. The other was her parents' great joy when, at last, they had a son. She therefore grew up believing in the unquestionable authority of the Church and developing a deep sense of girls being secondary to boys, beliefs that continued into adulthood and marriage. Then began a series of geographical moves which were also to bring gradual shifts in her perception of both the Church and herself.

'We were in Brussels and I was teaching religion to primary grades. Small children ask questions which are direct and profound. They want to know big and difficult things in simple terms.'

Alexina began to question too. In six years she had had four children and would have many more if she continued to follow the Church's teaching on contraception. Her sense of self-regard as a woman was in the balance. She underwent two years of psychoanalysis and found it to be a good growing experience. 'I became aware of how hurtful it had been that my brother had been so much more important than me and my sisters. Also, my parents were doing it again, making my husband more important than me. I had lost my identity. I was suffering from sexism and needed to name it.'

The family moved on to Toronto, and Alexina began five years of study for a degree in theology. It was during this period that she became an active feminist and soon after the family's return to England in the mid-eighties planned the weekend conference that was to be the beginning of the Catholic Women's Network, its purpose to look at women's experience in the Church.

'Not a lot of people know about us. We have a newsletter which comes out quarterly and goes to about 350 addresses. A typical Network member is thirty-six years old and married.'

This is the profile of Catholic women who now challenge their Church, who join together in liturgical celebration which they feel to be a Eucharist, although there is no male priest present and the venues are not officially hallowed. The women don't break bread; instead they pass grapes to one another and drink water. They want to avoid violating long-conditioned Eucharistic sensibilities. 'We are not too confronting,' says Alexina. 'We are not challenging areas we have not yet fully opened up and explored.'

'I don't think I would ever disengage from the parish – I could not call myself a practising Catholic if I did. I don't really believe in the separation of men and women. The biggest challenge is women and men together. Most men who are "with it" are in favour of women's ordination, just as they are of married clergy.'

Even so, Alexina says she would like to work only with women, to talk only with women; that women's community could be sufficient for her, and that continuing her attendance at parish Mass is largely so that she can worship with her husband, who is excluded from the women's groups.

'All the time I feel enraged and embittered by the Church. I still go because I do not know what to put in its place. The ordination of women must happen, but I don't see how it is going to happen. There are no official shifts towards letting it happen. It is only in the last few years that I have come to see that all the Churches have got to give something up in order to achieve something else. What happened at the Reformation was less disruptive than the issue of women's ordination. It is terribly dangerous for the Church to be living like this.'

Alexina and the Catholic women activists are not alone in recognising Rome's intransigence towards women as dangerous. On the day I went to see her, the *Catholic Herald* reported on the first draft of the American bishops' pastoral letter on women in the Church, following Rome's reaffirmation that the offices of lector or acolyte remain barred to women.

The letter, based on widespread consultation with women in 100 dioceses, 60 colleges and 45 military bases, came after persistent lobbying by us delegates at the 1987 Rome Synod for the abolition of 'the sin of sexism' from the structures and laws of the Church.

'The sin of sexism should be recognised for what it is, and attitudes tending towards it, or an incapacity to deal with women as equals, should be considered as negative indications for fitness for ordination,' it reads, and goes on to call for women to be admitted to the male ministries of reader, acolyte and altar-server, and for reasons for barring women to the priesthood to be re-examined.

'We regret and confess our individual and collective failures to respond to women as they deserve. We call the people of God to join us in personal and corporate contrition of the sins of sexism that violate the basic tenets of our faith,' the letter concludes.

The Synod took place shortly after the Pope's much-publicised visit to the United States in September 1987, and while it was said by the Archbishop of San Francisco that trying to measure the impact of the Pope's tour was like attempting to measure the beauty of the sunset, there were also clouds in the sky. As is so often the case, and it happened in San Francisco, the causes of women, homosexuals and the divorced were repeatedly lumped together. Noisy protests took place and the aggrieved, prefacing their appeals with acknowledgement of the Church as a non-democratic authority, nonetheless demanded acceptance, equality and human rights.

The Pope kept more or less silent on the subject, waiting, it seems, until he got back to the Vatican and the Synod on the Laity, which took place in October 1987. However, he had told America's 52 million Catholics (although the Church was disappointed at the number who turned up to listen in each city) that dissent was not compatible with being a good Catholic, perhaps paving the way for what was to come from the Synod in its list of recommendations for papal approval.

As the three-week debate drew to a close there was every indication that the 216 cardinals and bishops from around the world would be recommending that women be allowed to perform every ecclesiastical function short of the priesthood – from altar-girl to papal diplomat. In addition, there was talk of re-examining the arguments against ordaining women.

Another week went by, during which the Synod was thought to be finalising its already drafted recommendations.

Then came the bombshell. At the end of October the final

propositions were made public and the clause concerning women was not among them. It had been thrown out by the Pope's advisers. Women were to be kept firmly in the pews and nowhere near the pulpit. The Pope's unequivocal opposition to women priests was clear, and support for his stance had arrived in the form of a 40,000-signature petition from conservative Catholic women in America and Europe. 'A woman cannot be a priest, just as a man cannot be a mother,' they said.

Britain's Cardinal Basil Hume, Archbishop of Westminster, was among what is thought to have been an overwhelming majority in favour of the clause for women. However, strict secrecy surrounded the Synod's proceedings and even if all 216 members had voted for the clause, the ultimate decision remained with the Pope, who sooner or later was due to issue an encyclical on the matter.

Certainly, the removal of the vital clause came as a surprise to Vatican-watchers, particularly as only two months earlier, at the end of August 1987, Pope John Paul had said that it was the right time to examine more deeply how to give women a broader share in the various sectors of the Church's apostolate. The *Tablet* reported:

> In a reference to the ordained priesthood, he said that 'women are
> not called to the type of mission which the Lord gave to the
> apostles as their own', but went on to stress that 'they are
> nevertheless vouchsafed roles of great importance in spreading the
> good news'. He drew attention to the increased contribution of
> women since Vatican II in evangelisation, catechesis, liturgy,
> theology and, generally speaking, in the Church's mission in the
> world.

Finally, the cardinals and bishops were allowed, at least, to publish their condemnation of discrimination against women; but this generalisation was mocked and contradicted by the very omission of the anti-discrimination clause.

Before leaving this section on the Catholics it is interesting to note the words of an earlier Pope, John XXIII. In a book entitled *The Question of Women and the Priesthood*, Sister Vincent Emmanuel Hannon recorded more than twenty years ago this extract from Pope John's encyclical *Pacem in Terris*:

It is obvious to everyone that women are now taking a part in public life. This is happening more rapidly perhaps in nations of Christian civilisation, and more slowly, but broadly, among peoples who have inherited other traditions or cultures. Since women are becoming ever more conscious of their human dignity, they will not tolerate being treated as mere material instruments, but demand rights befitting a human person both in domestic and in public life.

The present Pope's missive on the dignity of women, completed in the autumn of 1988, has been dismissed as anachronistic and largely unintelligible; but this could be because it is written in Latin.

The Nonconformists

In the Rev. Ruth Matthews's office at the Church of the Resurrection in Hemel Hempstead there is a cartoon stuck on the wall: the Church of England is talking about women's ordination again and wants to know God's opinion. 'Oh no, not again – tell them I'm busy, comes the reply. 'I'm sorry,' relays an angel. 'She's busy.'

Ruth Matthews has been a Baptist minister for twenty-five years. She is also the Ecumenical Officer for Hertfordshire and Bedfordshire and the Diocesan Officer on ecumenical matters for the Anglicans. There is nothing particularly unusual in any of this, but within the Church of the Resurrection and Mrs Matthews's ministry there is something going on that is just about as radical as can be in the mainstream of church life.

The Grovehill area of Hemel Hempstead is a massive housing estate with a population of 12,000, and when the Baptists, Anglicans and Roman Catholics decided to build churches to serve this new community the ecumenical thing to do was a joint venture – one church to be shared between the three congregations. It began a decade ago and has meant sharing resources, social events and, in the case of the Baptists and the Anglicans, Sunday services, although none of it has been strictly 'legal' within the canons of the Church of England.

A normal Sunday at the Church of the Resurrection begins with nine-thirty Mass followed by coffee, followed by the eleven o'clock

Baptist/Anglican service. The arrangement is that every first and third Sunday in the month the service is basically Anglican, and every second and fourth basically Baptist. The church itself has been cleverly designed to incorporate all the requirements of each denomination's rituals, so that the Stations of the Cross adorn the walls in tapestry, while sunk into the flooring is a deep bath for total-immersion baptism.

I had arranged to meet Ruth Matthews to find out about her experiences as a woman minister, but much of the time I spent with her we talked about this incredible sharing experiment which, ultimately, might be considered as central to the debate on women's ordination and the supposed threat it poses to unity.

'In theory, the Roman Catholics who share this Church do not see me as ordained, but some call me 'Reverend Ruth' because they want to give me a title, and there are a couple of feminists who consciously like me being a minister,' she said.

More pertinent is her position with the Anglicans. As the Baptist congregation's minister she takes the eleven o'clock service every other Sunday and because Baptist liturgy is not set she can choose to use the Anglican form. She can preside at the Eucharist, lead the Anglicans through a 'recognised' service and be recognised herself as a 'priest' in a way no Anglican woman deacon could on the first and third Sundays or any other time or place within the Church of England. She could, if she chose, invite an Anglican woman deacon or overseas-ordained priest to preside at a 'basically Baptist' shared service, but that would be mischievous and a threat to the delicate structure of co-operation which has proved workable in Grovehill.

Ruth says she has been accepted by her colleagues and their parishioners in the other denominations because she is not a priest and therefore not a threat to Catholic and Anglican tradition. Baptist ministers, be they women or men, are just that; their ordination sets them aside for a particular task, making their office 'function'-orientated as opposed to 'status'-orientated, which is the perception of priesthood. 'Because I am not a priest, but a minister, I find this "teases" out those who are prejudiced against women and those who have a real theological stumbling-block.'

In her work as Diocesan Officer she has met resistance to her 'minister' status. There are those, particularly in the High churches of Anglicanism who have found it impossible to introduce her to their congregations as the 'Reverend' Ruth Matthews; and like many ordained women I have spoken to, she does not push her title. She feels that she could not effectively carry out her job if she was overtly feminist, although she is constantly working to give women equal opportunities in the ecumenical movement, and in the liturgy she is known for her muttering of 'and women' when non-inclusive language is used by colleagues.

Throughout her career she has been largely cushioned from hard-line prejudice. 'The Baptist system protects you from the worst of it. If a church won't have a woman there is no way they will ever get one. You only get invited to places where the majority want you.'

Perhaps the single most telling example of prejudice from her own denomination happened when she decided to get married. Writing about Ruth in her book *A Map of the New Country*, Sara Maitland explains:

> Although Baptists have no tradition of celibate pastors, and indeed react strongly against this, she was the first Baptist professional in the English Baptist Union who had ever proposed staying on at work after getting married. After training she worked in a parish as the assistant minister; when she told her senior that she was planning to get married he said, 'I thought you had given up that sort of thing.' He found it difficult . . . because apparently he could only see me as a minister if I was some kind of sexless person, or at least de-sexed – some kind of 'set apart virgin female'.
>
> This kind of de-sexing of ordained women as a subtle form of sexual discrimination is very common. Ruth Matthews was once asked by an official Baptist panel if when she was in the pulpit she saw herself 'more as a woman or as a minister' when she preached, as though the two were incompatible and she had to make some sort of choice. On her marriage, to another Baptist minister, she was obliged to leave her denomination's pension scheme despite her declared commitment to continuing in the ministry.

The Matthews ministered in neighbouring parishes, living in his while she commuted to hers, and when their children were born they took on a joint ministry. She told me:

'I was expected to give up when the children came so they wouldn't suffer. I didn't and they haven't. They seem to enjoy having a mother as a minister more than they did a father [John Matthews has now left the ministry] – it is less authoritarian. People will say that the office is diminished if the authoritarian nature is taken away, but a man who makes it authoritarian will already have diminished it.'

The authoritarian nature of ministry is of course rooted in sexism, and liberal theological thinking, however egalitarian in theory, will for a very long time to come be up against the prejudice of a male-dominated society. Even the Free Churches, most of which ordain women and, in the case of the Baptists, have done so for most of this century, in practice still discriminate between the sexes. As Gill Barker wrote in a recent issue of *Baptist Times*:

> Until everyone is free to contribute his or her own particular gifts and insights, without the gender tag getting in the way, we haven't got our act together as well as we might imagine. But hands up any Baptist who hasn't felt just the merest twinge of complacency whenever public airing is given to the Church of England's continuing debate on the ordination of women. We confidently think that we have long since seen the light on that issue, and there is no problem about the role of the women who constitute one half of our denomination.
>
> Please think again. How is it that in some churches the anachronism of an all-male diaconate continues to be tolerated? Why are women so under-represented at regional and national level? Why are there no women superintendents? . . . And just how many of our churches would genuinely consider appointing a woman to their pastorates, however well-qualified she may be? Are we really so enlightened after all?

The Baptists had 'She-fellow-labourers' who preached in Cromwellian times, and yet there are many Fundamentalist congregations today who would not allow a woman to preach or minister to them.

'This is hearsay,' says Ruth Matthews, 'but I have been told that there are more women ministering to inner-city churches because they will go where the men won't. It's exhausting in those areas and the suggestion is that women are more committed. It could be the case that women are the second choice.'

Indeed it could. After almost seventy years of ordaining women, the Baptists currently list about seventy accredited women ministers among two thousand men. In the United Reformed Church one in ten of their ministers is a woman, but they began ordaining women before the First World War (or rather, their forerunners, the Congregationalists, did). The Presbyterians, now part of the United Reformed Church, decided that it was a reasonable idea in the 1920s but delayed action until the 1950s, when the first Presbyterian woman was ordained. However, she was to be the sole representative of her sex for a further decade. The Methodists took the plunge in the early 1970s, and perhaps are the least sexist in that they have been reported as 'recognising only ministers', and not their gender, when asked to list them.

Returning to the Baptists, who, because of the length of time they have been ordaining women and the continuity of the denomination, have had more experience than most of the Free Churches, it is worth mentioning the findings of a recent study into their attitudes to women ministers.

This was carried out in the UK by American Sociology Professor Edward Lehman, himself a Baptist. According to the *Baptist Times*, he received 360 responses to his questionnaire and from these concluded that the church member most likely to accept a woman minister has the following profile: she is an older woman with little money, whose fellow church members have unskilled, low-prestige occupations. She feels the Church ought to be heavily involved in helping those who cannot help themselves and trying to reform the structures of society. She is a member of a small struggling church in a small community.

At the other end, the Professor's study profiled the Church member most likely to oppose women in ministry: this is a young man earning a fairly high salary in a high-status occupation. He is a regular churchgoer and thinks the Church should be heavily into evangelism. He is not much interested in social reform or helping the helpless. His church is in a large city with a large, growing congregation.

Professor Lehman says churches are 'fragile voluntary organisations' in which members must be persuaded and cajoled into accepting structural and cultural innovations; and, concurring with Ruth Matthews's 'hearsay' comment, he says that small churches are more inclined to accept a woman minister because they have to.

The findings of this study have not been accepted as anywhere near accurate by British Baptists, who have said that it is more often women who do not want women, and that the churches which have called women ministers are not, on average, among the denomination's smaller churches. Nevertheless, the *Baptist Times* article, from which I have culled much of this information on the study and reaction to it concludes:

> Many of our women ministers who served first as deaconesses, and were later recognised as ministers, shared the experience, which one put like this: 'We often did the work of the minister in starting a church in a council estate, only to be moved on when the work built up and the church was able to support a minister. We knew it would happen. It led to sadness but seldom bitterness.'

The Orthodox Church

'If we could get rid of priesthood as a vocation, it would be better. Personal vocation is for monks and nuns,' says Dr Elizabeth Briere, a Devon-born member of the Orthodox Church, and Secretary of the Fellowship of St Alban and St Sergius, which maintains dialogue between Orthodox and Western Christians.

The Orthodox Church claims to be the third largest Christian denomination in Britain. Worldwide, it has around 250 million followers and, according to Dr Briere, the ordination of women is not an issue, although she concedes that it is given some thought in the United States if not elsewhere in the Orthodox world.

Understanding Orthodoxy is difficult for outsiders; the Orthodox Church itself says that it sees the world and humanity differently from other religions. Tradition is all important, yet this doesn't mean that change is impossible, just unlikely.

'What role is there for a woman in the Orthodox Church?' Elizabeth Briere posed this question in a recent paper published in the London Russian Orthodox Cathedral newsletter. She writes that those disillusioned with traditional Orthodox societies say that: 'The Church is male-dominated – it's an irrelevance for a modern woman,' while others in similar societies say: 'We clean the church, we bake the prosfora, we look after the lamps – there are plenty of things for us to do in the Church, so there is no need for anything to change.' Neither answer is likely to satisfy those Orthodox women who do, very definitely, feel that they belong in the Church, but are genuinely perplexed by so many of the attitudes to women which have existed and persist within it. They find themselves at a loss to sort out what really belongs to the tradition of the Church and what has simply reflected unregenerate human prejudice.

This does not sound so very different to the dichotomy confronting the Church of England, although in the Orthodox Church, tradition goes a lot further than keeping women from the priesthood: even today, it keeps them physically out of church immediately after childbirth and during menstruation, when they are considered to be ritually unclean. Dr Briere admits that this restriction is offensive and incomprehensible to many women and, quite obviously, would create practical difficulties for an ordained woman.

The position of women in the Orthodox Church is, without doubt, further away from the altar than in any other mainstream Christian denomination, but their role among the laity depends largely on the society in which they live. For instance, in Greece, the women look after their church in practical ways but are rarely elected to the parish committees, whereas in the Russian diocese of London women are active on the diocesan assembly.

'It is not a very clerical Church,' says Dr Briere. 'A lot is done by the laity. The problem in many places is that women don't take their full place in the laity. This is particularly the case in Russia, where the official spokesperson would always be a man, although Russian women are now being trained as 'choirmasters' and religious education teachers – many more women, in fact, than men.

'In my own diocese women are not underused, and this doesn't mean the rules have been bent or that anybody has been surprised. It is very disconcerting, very worrying, that people think that if you are committed to the Church you have to want to be ordained. It is more difficult for men because the assumption is that they have to be ordained if committed, when this might not be the best way for them as individuals.'

Dr Briere says that 99.9 per cent of Orthodox Christians, of both sexes, would see equality in priesthood as irrelevant and yet there are moves within the Church to restore the ancient order of deaconesses, and surely this is the route by which women in the Church of England have come. Orthodoxy, like other denominations and religions which deny priesthood to women, strenuously denies that it is a sexist issue, although the criterion for ordination among men in the Orthodox Church is peculiarly sexist in itself. For instance, a eunuch cannot be a priest; neither can a priest marry, although a married man can become a priest, but not if he or his wife have been divorced.

'In practice, priesthood is a vocation,' Dr Briere told me, explaining her earlier comment, 'but that is not what it should be about. It is no big deal. Mostly priests are full-time, but in Greece, in the past, the parish clergy were not people with great education; they could be farmers and would carry on farming.

'The ordination of women is not a live issue for us. I don't know whether, in the fullness of time, Orthodoxy will admit women. I think it is something that needs to be thought about seriously with a long-term view, looking back over the whole tradition of the Church, but I don't know what might emerge.'*

So what about the Anglican priests who threaten to leave a Church of England with women priests and go to Orthodoxy or Rome?

'The Orthodox Church has been approached by ordained and laity fleeing the Church of England, but this is not what Orthodoxy is about. Not liking the way the Church of England is going is no reason to be Orthodox. It is not an old-guard Anglican Church.'

* Since this interview with Dr Briere, the Orthodox Churches, in November 1988, held a major international consultation in Rhodes to discuss the role of women in the Church. Out of this gathering has come a recommendation to revive the order of deaconesses.

Much as Dr Briere and others might deny that the ordination of women is a 'live' issue in Orthodoxy, there are, of course, those who disagree. Anglicans, if they were to 'flee' to Orthodoxy, would in a sense make it an issue, and in a book of essays, *Women and the Priesthood*, editor Thomas Hopko concludes that it is the issue of our time. However, he says that the Orthodox Church has hardly begun to formulate its response to this issue, even though it knows what it believes and practises concerning men and women in the life of the Church, including the priesthood 'but it appears certain that it will take years of theological labour for her [the Church] to arrive at a fitting dogmatic statement to explain and defend it'.

This is an American view, but in recent months the focus has been on Russia and for many women there must seem a degree of irony in the new freedom Mikhail Gorbachev has proclaimed for members of the Orthodox Church (as well as other denominations and religions) – an equality that, to an outsider, is not reflected within the Church itself.

The Jews

When I went to meet Rabbi Jacqueline Tabick at the West London Synagogue I showed her, as I have done most of the people I've interviewed, the synopsis for this book. It included a canon's words about women's ordination – 'a can of worms better left in the bottom of the boat' – which made Rabbi Tabick laugh and, quick as a flash, counter: 'If you leave the can of worms at the bottom of the boat you will never catch any fish.'

Rabbi Tabick, married to a rabbi and mother of two young sons, was the first woman in Britain to be ordained into the rabbinate. This was in 1975, just two years after America was first, with Rabbi Sally Priestland; although it is believed that a woman was ordained privately in Germany in 1939, dying soon afterwards in a Nazi concentration camp.

The difference between Rabbi Tabick and Rabbi Priestland is that the American is part of the mainstream Progressive movement, while Rabbi Tabick is in the very small minority of Liberal and

Reform Jews in the UK and remains unrecognised by the hundreds of thousands of British Orthodox Jews. She is one of only half a dozen women rabbis, and even within the liberal community to which she belongs there are many synagogues where she would not be accepted. The same biblical texts which are applied by Christians opposing women priests are cited by Jews who believe it is improper for women to be rabbis.

'It's not even on the horizon for the Orthodox,' Rabbi Tabick explained. 'It's not possible within the law. Women cannot lead services where men are present.'

The role of a rabbi is to teach and to judge, and in Orthodox Judaism no woman could perform either function over a man, although they are allowed to lead other women and have just begun to be admitted on to synagogue boards or councils. This said, throughout the history of the Jews there have always been prominent women, usually the wives of rabbis, famed for the support they gave to their husbands – although in the late eighteenth century, in the early Hassidic movement, there was a woman who preached sermons.

It was in Germany in the mid-nineteenth century that liberal principles came to the fore, although it would be another hundred years before women achieved a position approaching equality in the rabbinate. 'The Progressive movement declared equality in the middle of the nineteenth century,' says Rabbi Tabick, 'but the background of prejudice delayed the first women rabbis. Religion is always behind the rest of society – it's a more deep-rooted thing.'

Jewish law is enshrined in the first five books of Moses, the Torah, and Orthodox believers say that this is God-given and not open to change. Progressives believe in re-interpretation according to the times in which we live, and in the late twentieth century this means there is an opportunity to proclaim women.

Rabbi Tabick grew up in an atmosphere of opportunity. Her girlhood synagogue in Ilford had a strong tradition of equality and by the age of fifteen she was regularly leading services – a role traditionally open to the laity in Judaism, which, of course, has no sacrament equivalent to the Eucharist.

As a lay-reader it was a natural progression that took her towards ordination, but she shied away from being the first woman rabbi in Britain: 'I was hoping that someone would get there before me – I didn't want to be first. Look at Rabbi Julia Neuberger, then look at me – I'm not a media person.'

She delayed the process by taking a history degree at London University, then a teaching diploma in Manchester, before applying for a place at the Leo Baeck College which trains all rabbis in the Liberal and Reform movements. But prejudice went with her application form as it passed from one desk to another within the college. It seemed impossible that a woman could read Hebrew, that a woman could have the intellect required for the rabbinate. Action was delayed for as long as possible but once she was 'in', one of only six candidates for her year, there was to be a lot of support from both staff and fellow students.

'Even so, I always felt I had to achieve more than anyone else to justify my position. I was the only person at that time who, by the end, had fulfilled every single criterion to become a rabbi.'

When she finished college she was appointed education officer at the West London Synagogue, but had to wait another two years before she became a rabbi – two years longer than would have been the case had she been a man.

'I think, in a sense, my approach was right. I had made a decision that I was not going to fight. I think it is counterproductive, that it increases opposition. I wanted to get there without the rows. "Softly, softly, catchy monkey" was my approach, and it worked here. For instance, for many years I performed very few funerals. The relatives didn't want me and this was very hurtful when I had been visiting them. But as I have become known it has become preferable to have "the lady who is known" rather than a man who is not.'

There have always been pockets of resistance, and in her early days at West London there was a man in the congregation who overtly read a newspaper if Rabbi Tabick was taking the service. 'You do get hurt sometimes, but there is the other side, and since I have been here there has been a dramatic increase in the number of

girls coming for *bat mitzvah* [the female equivalent of *bar mitzvah*]
and the number of women in leadership roles — we now have a
woman chairman and a woman warden, which would have been
unheard of years ago. The thing is, women are so well-organised. I
have this theory that if women undertake work outside the home
they have to be very well-organised.'

Her own situation demands good organisation. She works a
sixty-hour week, much of the time in the evenings and at weekends,
and yet she feels that such 'crazy' hours are, in a strange way, easier
for a woman. 'We have an au pair for the children, but I can arrange
things so that I am at home for the vital hours — when they come in
from school. And when they were babies they came with me. This
building is full of children anyway and having mine with me often
gave people an excuse to come and see me. Once I'd had babies I
was "all right"; I was "normal" and no longer a threat.'

However much Rabbi Tabick may have broken down the old
prejudices, she knows it is unlikely that she will ever become the
senior rabbi at West London or any other synagogue in Britain.
Younger men will be appointed over her, and there is even the
possibility that women will lose ground.

'The "right" wing is growing because people want certainty — to
be told rather than to be allowed to question. It is happening in all
religions. Maybe people feel too vulnerable in the modern world.'

Orthodox extremists speak out with no holds barred. Jewish
schoolchildren are being told that women rabbis have caused AIDS
because their being ordained is immoral and has brought forth the
wrath of God. Polarisation is predicted, with the 'centre' shrinking
as the 'right' and 'left' grow, and in this movement there is the
danger that women will be sacrificed. At the moment there are
more women students at Leo Baeck than there are men, and protest
is beginning to be heard. The college is funded by the congregations
and a large number, however progressive in other matters, would
not accept a woman rabbi — which means that many of the women
currently studying will have nowhere to go.

'There is a feeling that the job has been 'downgraded' and fewer
men feel it is a man's place,' Rabbi Tabick says. 'This will keep the

wages down and there will be more part-timers. Over 60 per cent of rabbis leave the full-time rabbinate ten years after they have come out of college. The career structure is not good for men or women, but we are worried now that we might be pushed out.'

Even Rabbi Tabick, positioned as she is in a synagogue largely led and run by women, is considering her future. She and her husband are talking about going to America, even though neither of them wants to leave the UK.

The Muslims

When I began to make enquiries about Islam and the position of modern Muslim women within their religion I was warned against approaching my research with the bias of Western methodology. 'There is a lot of misrepresentation — the stereotypical view from the West that Muslim women are oppressed,' Muslim theologian Rashida Sharif told me.

Rashida Sharif was born in Pakistan and came to Britain when she was seven. She has a degree in English from Birmingham University and taught English for four years before taking up a post-graduate degree in Islamic studies and gaining an MA in theology. She is now an adviser for multi-cultural education in the West Midlands. A practising Muslim, married to an English Muslim, she is a prominent speaker on the role of women in Islam and is also a member of a women's committee within the British Council of Churches.

There are about 600 million Muslims spread throughout the world, and according to Rashida Sharif there is no such thing in Islam as MOW, and the question is not 'why not?', but 'why should there be?'

To understand this, the Westerner brought up in the Christian faith has to go back to the roots of Islam, roots that are funda-mentally different for womankind when compared with the Adam and Eve story of the Old Testament. In Islam men and women have always been equal, woman was not made from a man's rib, but the two sexes were created from a single pot of blood and then assigned their different, but equal, roles.

The five 'pillars' of Islam which dictate how a Muslim will live apply equally to men and women, but take account of women's physiological condition. For instance, during Ramadan, the month of fasting, a woman who is pregnant or menstruating is exempt. The traditional Islamic view of menstruation is again different from that of the Christians and Jews: women are not 'unclean' during this time and have never been viewed as such.

To the outsider, the Islamic rituals of prayer, fasting and pilgrimage might appear rigid and over-demanding, but all are tempered with practicality. Intention is what counts, and intent is a private matter between the individual and God.

Briefly, the five pillars are: Shahada – the declaration of faith; Zakat – the giving of a net percentage of income; Ramadan; Haj – the once-in-a-lifetime pilgrimage to Mecca; and, what seems the least practical, prayer five times a day preceded by triple washing or ablution. All apply equally to men and women, although a woman with young children to look after may be exempt from the regular prayer ritual.

Where Islam begins to appear to discriminate against its women is inside the mosque. The sexes are segregated to avoid mutual distraction, but it is always the women who are behind the men. Perfectly practical, argues Rashida Sharif: some of the attitudes of prayer involve bending, a position uncomfortable for a woman if she knows there is a man standing behind her. For the same reason, Muslim women throughout the world wear long skirts. Again, inside the mosque, it is always a man who will lead prayer; he is not the equivalent of an ordained Christian priest, but simply someone of good character and standing in the community who is given the title Imam.

Surely there must be modern Muslim women somewhere in the world who, like some modern Christian women, are demanding this 'priestly' position for their sex? 'No, why should they?' says Rashida Sharif. 'It is not their role. Why should they want it? It is not an issue.' She goes on to explain that every mosque is an educational establishment as well as a place for prayer, and that women and men are equally entitled to teach.

However, here lies the problem in modern Islam, a problem that is quite the reverse of that faced by many Christian women. 'Priesthood' does not exist in Islam, so, as Rashida says, there is no issue, nothing to parallel the Movement for the Ordination of Women; what does exist is a demand for equality in education so that Muslim women are equipped to fulfil their teaching vocation. The right is already theirs, enshrined in Islamic theology and tradition. It is the Islamic social structure of modern times that has worked against them, while in the West, changing social conditions have brought women to the brink of equality within a theological tradition that has never given them equivalent fundamental rights.

'There is a huge gap between theory and practice,' says Rashida. 'Muslim women have had a lot of their rights taken away by social structure. In terms of teaching, women and men have equal rights in Islam but socialisation has got in the way. This can be seen among Muslim women in Britian. It is in Egypt and Iran that women are now demanding all their rights and going to the Koran and finding out their "lost" rights.'

But surely she cannot be referring to those poor creatures we Westerners see in the Middle East with 'black bags' over their heads – seemingly willing victims of extremist revivalism as orchestrated by the Ayatollah Khomeini and his like? Now, of course, I am guilty of viewing this revival through the eyes of my Western upbringing. Rashida sighs. Talk of 'black bags' over female heads indicates a very superficial understanding of what it is all about. Those Muslim Fundamentalists in the Middle East have gone back to their 'black bags' – the *hijab* – with joy and relief as well as fervour. It is a sign of modesty, the Muslim woman's criterion for dress, and, as Rashida puts it, 'it keeps the men off'. Practicality again, but this last remark begs a great deal as to the equality of the sexes in Islam, and the fact remains that there are no women ayatollahs – the closest Muslims come to the priesthood.

'Muslim women have never been ones to talk about inferiority,' Rashida told me, 'they no longer wish to defend this position. European women have tended to say, "Here is the package – we have been through it, to get liberated," but Muslims have to fight in their own time and at their own pace.'

Not long after talking to Rashida Sharif, I met the secretary of the Islamic Society for the Promotion of Religious Tolerance in the UK. Zarina Choudry is English by birth and adopted Islam after her marriage to a Muslim. A few days after our meeting she kindly sent me a copy of the Koran, accompanied by a letter requesting that I keep the holy book in a clean high place and refrain from reading it while menstruating.

I wrote to Mrs Choudry, thanking her for sending me the Koran. I was going to leave it at that but the feminist in me added a comment of bewilderment over the, to me, unacceptable restriction on reading. A couple of days later Dr Hesham El-Essawy of the Society telephoned to tell me there was no such restriction, that it was merely a symptom of over-reverence on the part of some Muslim women. This seemed to explain why they are not ayatollahs, and that women in Islam, as in other religions, are restricting *themselves*.

The Sikhs

Like Islam, the Sikh religion does not in theory have a problem when it comes to the roles of men and women. They are equal, and as Sikhism has no priesthood the issue of women's ordination does not exist, and the struggles within the Anglican Church are viewed with, well, mild amusement.

Sikhism is the world's youngest mainstream religion. It was founded five hundred years ago by the first of the sect's ten gurus, Nanak, at a time when India was in turmoil, with Muslims holding the power and persecuting the Hindus. Sikhism was born out of Hinduism, in the same way as Christianity sprang from Judaism. Guru Nanak's message was that we are all God's children and therefore no community should consider itself superior to another, no individual consider themselves above another. He travelled more than 20,000 miles spreading this message, and today his teaching is followed by around 300,000 Sikhs in Britian, considerably outnumbering Hindus.

'Guru Nanak raised the whole question of the subordination of

women five hundred years ago,' prominent Sikh Charanjit Ajit
Singh told me. 'He saw what people engaged in war did to women
and he was very hurt by it, and the general persecution of all
humanity. He complained to God that humanity was terrorised, and
women in particular, having their dreams shattered and being
subjected to degradation. He asked God if he didn't feel pity. How
could women be called bad when they gave birth to kings? The
epitome of power at that period was man, but Nanak looked on
women as being more important.'

Charanjit Ajit Singh is a member of the Southall Sikh community
in West London. She is also involved with the British Council of
Churches and attends international gatherings of women from all
religions. By profession she is a senior adult education officer. She
dresses in traditional style and, like all true Sikhs, has never cut her
hair, which is considered part of the body and therefore sacred.
Sikhs lead as natural a life as possible, and until those now living in
Britain came to this country and were required to have surnames,
had abandoned the 'caste' names which denoted social standing.

'We are the most democratic of Churches,' Charanjit Ajit Singh
says. 'We are run by committee, and this is made up of men and
women. There is no problem with women's ordination for us.
Baptism is the nearest we have to ordination and that is for both
sexes and takes place when you are able to understand the religion.'

Yet can it be so perfectly egalitarian to be a Sikh? 'Theoretically
there is no inequality, but in practice there may be. Literacy has a
lot to do with it and men do control the temples in many cases; but
in this country there have been times when women have found that
men are not doing things properly and then the women have taken
control. In our religion the mothers, wives, sisters and daughters of
the gurus have shaped the faith. Sikhism brought the unveiling of
women, stopped girls being killed at birth, encouraged women to sit
in the temple, and got rid of Suttee [the ritual suicide of widows]
and allowed them to re-marry.' The Sikhs made these changes, but
in present-day India there are Hindus who still perpetrate such at-
rocities.

As well as the initial teachings of Nanak, Sikhism owes much of its attitude towards women to Bibi Bhani, daughter of the third guru, wife of the fourth and mother of the fifth. She is said to have changed the course of Sikh history, influencing her son, who gave the religion its holy book – the Granth, to be read by men and women from the temple pedestal – and was also instrumental in founding the Sacred Golden Temple at Amritsar. Bibi Bhani established the first girls' school, in the sixteenth century, as part of the new emphasis on educating women.

But Bibi Bhani, influential as she may have been, was not a guru herself. 'We do not have a hierarchical structure like the Christians,' Charanjit Ajit Singh explains. 'It was not the role of women to be gurus. [After the tenth guru the Sikhs decided they needed no more.] In practice Sikh women do not conduct weddings or funerals, but they could. The Granthi, those who do these things, are mostly men, but all rites can be performed by women. Sikh men and women have the same first names, there is no discrimination. A Sikh should be self-sufficient and able to conduct all services, so a woman can preach at the altar just as a man can. Sikhs refer to God as Father and Mother.'

Charanjit Ajit Singh admits that despite all the theoretical equality, in reality it is not quite so: 'But does equality mean doing the same thing or different things?' she asks. 'Women don't work on hierarchical levels.'

NINE

Fundamentalism – the big revival

'Spring Harvest', the annual Fundamentalist jamboree, attracted 30,000 bookings within five days of the 1989 reservations office opening, jamming the seventeen telephone lines set up by the organisers and even disrupting 999 emergency cover in one area. People in Britain are joining the Fundamentalists in droves.

In Cambridge, where I met the leaders of two Fundamentalist sects, congregations have grown in size over the past three or four years from half a dozen to several hundred, yet true Fundamentalism is no place for the emancipated woman. Leadership is almost exclusively male and the women seem to like it that way.

The Fundamentalists, not all of whom like to be given this label because of its somewhat sinister associations with extremist sects in America, take the Bible as 'gospel'. They believe it is without error and that it must be taken literally. This, of course, means that the much quoted passages from Timothy and Corinthians regarding the subservience of women are accepted as the irrefutable will of God. ('A woman must be a learner, listening quietly with due submission. I do not permit a woman to be a teacher, nor must woman domineer over man; she should be quiet.' (1 Timothy 2:11–12) 'And if they will learn anything, let them ask their husbands at home: for it is a shame for women to speak in the church.' (1 Corinthians 14:35)) Fundamentalism puts women equal before God, but not before man.

One of the most interesting aspects of these growing sects is their sexism and sudden popularity with both men and women at a time when the Church of England is attempting to rid itself of a sexist image. It rather looks as if a very large proportion of Christian women want to be led by men and don't want even the possibility of leadership for themselves or other women.

The Cambridge Christian Fellowship is a typical example of Fundamentalism today in England. It began in 1983–4 with six people. The originators had belonged to the Salvation Army and were joined by a couple of disillusioned Pentecostalists. They met in one another's homes for worship, but before long there were too many of them to continue in this way. A school hall had to be hired, and now membership is so large that the congregation has had to split in two to be accommodated.

Their leader, Tony Howson, still describes the Fellowship as a 'house church movement' and mid-week meetings are still held in members' homes, but if he has a problem it is space, an irony set against the empty pews of redundant churches in the Cambridge area.

Tony Howson was to have been an Anglican priest. He had been accepted for training and ordination when he decided that he was being led elsewhere. The direction he took initially was to become an ordained Pentecostal minister, but this proved not to be far enough for his beliefs. 'I left because the structuring was wrong. There was unity of name but not of spirit. I realised that unity did not come from labels.'

Tony is a pleasant, lucid man who told me he wanted to sound like a sensible person. Not unexpectedly, he interpolates Bible references every now and then, unhindered by the circumspection of Anglicanism.

'In the house church movement we have the priesthood of all believers, we are all priests, God has ordained all of us, but women would not be seen as "elders", and "elders" carry the authority. When Paul writes about forbidding a woman to teach, he is talking about authority.

'The position of women – Proverbs 31 – is one of marvellous

freedom, but always within the parameters of her authority, which is over her own children in her own home, but not over the Church. My wife is very glad that she doesn't have the responsibilities that I have. A woman can lead a small home group provided she does so within the authority of the Church. My wife is very closely involved in the Church and she has a ministry in her own right, but if something difficult comes up she will check with me first. We aren't equal – not in our function in the Church.'

As far as ministry is concerned, Tony says that, unlike Anglicans, he would have no problem with a woman ministering the sacraments and presiding at the Eucharist, always providing she does so within an exclusively masculine authority of the Church.

He believes the Church of England has got its structure and terminology all wrong, and if he was asked to take it over he says he would tear it apart, close all the churches and in fifteen years there would be the biggest revival in Christianity this country has ever seen. 'The whole point of Christian experience is security. People want no fudging of the issues, they want clarity and authority. The Church is not a democracy. I would have great difficulty going along with people like the Bishop of Durham who deny the virgin birth. Light cannot have fellowship with darkness. It is very easy to build up a church of cynics. Once I had seen the light I could never go back.'

Tony's Church is what he calls the 'Trans-Church', adhering to apostolic authority in the fashion of St Paul, who sent out others to spread the faith. 'Essentially it is a man's world in the Trans-Church world,' he says. 'The elders in the local church have this authority and they are called to rule.'

In spite of this pronouncement, he says the Church has always been ahead of the rest of society in recognising women – 'that is, until the very superficial feminist age of the 1970s'. So are there any women who leave his Church over the equality issue? He says not, that those who do go leave over 'authority', over the way the church is run.

Pastor Peter Mills, who leads another Fundamentalist sect in Cambridge, says he knows of no women who have left his Church over the equality issue either. Like Tony Howson, Peter Mills's manner is pleasant, open and reasonable and with nothing of the tyrannical evangelism the word 'Fundamentalist' has come to represent. Pastor Mills's Church is housed in a smart new chapel, built and paid for by his congregation in just three years. It is sited on Cambridge's largest housing estate, spotted by the Christian Brethren, an offshoot of the Plymouth Brethren, as churchless a few years back. They moved in and quickly developed a following strong enough to warrant the chapel.

Unlike Tony Howson, Peter Mills is ill at ease with the label 'Fundamentalist'. 'It conjures up pictures of us Fundamentalism, with overtones of right-wing politics,' he says and prefers the description 'evangelical'.

Traditionally, the Christian Brethren have no formal Church ministry but leadership by groups of laymen. 'Teaching is performed by males. Where women are used it is more as social workers. Through our understanding of the Scriptures we have a place for women's ministry – in the Communion Service they can get up and speak, but they cannot teach'. Here Peter Mills injects the well-worn quote from Timothy, permitting no woman to teach or have authority over men. 'This is the way things are. We try and move along happily. We have Bible study groups and ladies can contribute, but they are still formally led by men.'

The Arbury Chapel regularly attracts seventy or more worshippers on Sunday mornings and Peter Mills believes it is authority that is pulling them in, the same certainty in scriptural truth that is swelling the numbers in Tony Howson's house church movement and new evangelical sects throughout the country. But why this sudden upsurge in Fundamentalism? Is it the same desire for certainty and authority that elects a right-wing government? Tony Howson feels there is a connection, that Fundamentalism and capitalism are both God's way, most aptly demonstrated in the parable of the talents. That the Fundamentalists don't appear fully to apply this parable to the talents of women is something of a puzzle, but it would seem that the women themselves are happy to accept their limitations as dictated elsewhere in the Bible.

Maybe the 'very superficial' feminist era of the 1970s brought too much too quickly and the new popularity of Fundamentalism is a symptom of retreat. In the Church of England evangelical theological colleges now have more than 50 per cent of the male candidates for ordination, but as yet there are insufficient evangelical parishes to accommodate them all. Whether the colleges are ahead of the parishes remains to be seen, but if they are, does this indicate the decline of liberal Anglicanism and all that goes with it, including the ordination of women? Chief among the liberals, the Archbishop of Canterbury himself has consistently warned against rushing the fences, perhaps recognising the post-feminist age as one of egalitarian uncertainty. He has been criticised as lacking authority and, regardless of whether or not such criticism is justified, the fact that it has been made is further evidence of the current desire for reactionary didactic leadership. In his posthumously published pamphlet 'Tradition and change in the Church' Gareth Bennett wrote:

> The real danger to the unity of the Church lies not in the existence
> of controversy but in a recalcitrant unwillingness on either side to
> accept the mind of the Church as it emerges. If a development is
> 'received' there needs to be some formulation of it by appropriate
> public authority so that it may be accepted as a norm to be acted
> upon and no longer be a source of discord.

This idea of 'change with authority' is very much the Fundamentalist way. Change means getting closer to God's pattern as set out in the Bible, according to Tony Howson's wife Margaret. Like her husband, she grew up in the Anglican Church but became dissatisfied with its liberal ways. 'I was increasingly unhappy about the Church of England, but it was a total shock to me when I realised that our vicar was not a born-again Christian, that he did not know God.'

Margaret is hugely enthusiastic about God. She says she knew in her early twenties that all she wanted to do with her life was to serve Him, and yet it never occurred to her that she might seek ordination. As she and Tony moved away from Anglicanism and embraced Fundamentalism it was always Tony who was asked to lead. 'I never thought I should be asked, I feel we have always both been called by God, but Tony should have the title even though we share the ministry. I am happy to have found my place in the body of Christ. It's not equal opportunities – I can't be an elder, but it doesn't bother me. I don't want that authority. I don't want to be answerable to God for all those things. I prefer my husband to have that responsibility.'

Before her work in the Church became full-time, Margaret was a physical education teacher. I asked her how she would have felt if she had been passed over for promotion because of her sex. 'I would have been up in arms about it,' she admits, so how can she accept job discrimination in her current occupation? Aside from the eternal authority of Scripture with its many passages indicating man's headship over woman, Margaret did not dismiss the post-feminist theory that the late twentieth-century woman is perhaps a different creature from the 1970s activist. The desire for authority isn't just a matter of looking for the will of God, and one of the appeals of Fundamentalism could be its unequivocal stance on the man-woman relationship.

In the United States, Fundamentalism is part of everyday life. Switch on the television at just about any time of the day or night and there will be someone shouting that we are all miserable sinners bound for hell fire and damnation – unless . . .

Among the many people I talked to in the States there was general acceptance that Fundamentalism is where Christianity is booming. 'It is a reaction to the great liberal period of our nation which has bankrupted us,' the Rev. Yvonne Delk, Executive Director of the United Church of Christ, told me. 'The Fundamentalists are attempting to thwart the movement of women by talking about family values and calling us back to the idea of men being at the head and women having a submissive role. I affirm the call back to motherhood and the family but it must be wider than that for women. What is happening is born out of fear, which is why there is a desire for a controlled world that does not allow for differences.'

Yvonne Delk's church, which is similar to the United Reformed in Britain, claims to have been the first to ordain a woman, Antoinette Brown Blackwell in 1853, and yet the UCC appears to be no further forward in its proportion of women clergy to men than the American Anglicans with their decade of women priests. Prejudice is still noticeable when parishes come to select new ministers, and the Rev. Delk considers that the women's movement within her Church has still to 'peak'.

Meanwhile, she sees the hard-line Fundamentalists as a serious threat in American society, even though some sects are breaking away and ordaining women. She reports that the Fundamentalists are moving in on farming people who have been experiencing economic problems in recent years, and their fear and vulnerability is being harnessed into extremist right-wing religious fervour. Blacks are already suffering, termed 'mud' people created as a result of broken covenants with God, and there is concern that women ministers will be persecuted on similar grounds.

No such threat seems likely in Britain, but Tony Howson says his Church is seen as a threat by local Anglicans in the 'pew-robbing' sense, and this is a threat that he relishes.

TEN

No
longer if,
but when?

Throughout my research, and talking with people of all shades of opinion, it has been clear that everyone believes women will be ordained to the priesthood one day. Even the Roman Catholics and the Orthodox Churches cannot rule out the possibility, but almost certainly theirs will be a much longer process. For the Church of England it could happen in just two or three years, and to the general public in Britain it must seem as if this will be the case. In fact many non-Church people think women are already 'vicars'; they see women wearing the clerical collar, and the distinction between deacon and priest is meaningless to those outside the Church. They have heard the Archbishop of Canterbury say that it is right and proper for women to be priests, and they have heard reported on the BBC Nine O'Clock News that the July 1988 General Synod voted in favour. To go further, and understand that, while the Archbishop has declared himself in favour, he voted against in Synod, and that the Synod, although voting positively, could still. reverse this decision, must be beyond the comprehension of those who are not familiar with the complex procedures which govern the workings of the Church of England.

The big moment, the one which captured the headlines, was at the beginning of July 1988 when the General Synod partially gathered up its skirts and the historic vote was taken that 'it shall be lawful for the General Synod to make provision by canon for enabling a woman to be ordained to the office of priest', some thirteen years after its decision that there were no fundamental objections to the ordination of women. The 1975 vote has, of course, proved a nonsense over the intervening years, as it became abundantly clear that there were, and still are, fundamental objections – and from a sizeable minority of bishops, priests and lay people. And the July 1988 vote, although it sounded historic, was only the first of a dozen or so further stages that have to be passed through and won, if women are to be ordained, at the earliest, in 1992.

These stages include revision, referral to the dioceses, final General Synod approval (with two-thirds majorities in each of the three Houses – Bishops, Clergy and Laity), more referral, then Parliamentary approval and Royal Assent. A 'no' vote at any of these stages would put the whole issue back for years: it could not come before the General Synod again until 1995 and the long, drawn-out process of revision and referral would have to start again from scratch.

To many in the Church, this latter course seems more and more likely. Between now and 1992 a new General Synod will have been elected (they are elected every five years), and there are strong indications that it will be more conservative than the present assembly. As things stand, the existing Synod has reduced its percentage of votes in favour of women priests compared with the voting in 1984 and 1987; although this reduction in the majority vote could have been a result of the Synod heeding Dr Runcie rather than an indication that fewer people want women priests.

In July 1988, as the nation's television screens were filled with the smiling faces of women deacons – all wearing their collars – confident that they were entering the 'home run', the grass-roots forces of the Association for the Apostolic Ministry had already been at work, marshalling the formidable opposition awakening in the parishes after centuries of largely unaltered tradition. No issue since the Reformation was so set to rock the format of faith, to bring forth the raging reactionaries, those who could not contemplate receiving Communion bread and wine consecrated by a woman; because this is what it had boiled down to – the Eucharist and Absolution are the only remaining sacraments unholy in the hands of women.

The week General Synod took its vote, AAM took eight pages in the form of a newsletter in each of the two leading Church of England publications, the *Church Times* and the *Church of England Newspaper*. It published the result of its own survey of clerical opinion, revealing that 12,028 clergy had been sent the questionnaire, 8,780 had responded and, while 39 per cent were in favour of women priests, 28 per cent were against, with the rest either mildly in favour, mildly opposed or undecided. The questionnaire went further. The clergy had been asked to consult their parishes, and while there were more in favour than against, the 'anti' parishes amounted to over 25 per cent, with a large proportion undecided. In addition, more than 1,000 of the 'anti' priests stated that they would not consider themselves in communion with a bishop who ordained women. The message and the threat was undeniable – schism, and on a scale foreseen by the Archbishop when he declared himself in favour of the principle but opposed to the practical reality at a time and within a climate of opinion that would bring pain and disunity unprecedented in the history of Anglicanism.

Glimpses of what might be to come could be found throughout the eight pages put together by AAM. Much as they might have attempted to hide it, there was the fear of eventual defeat and within this a degree of paranoia. In a piece headed 'The Ordination of Women Legislation – a first look at the measures and canons' Canon Brian Brindley suggested that in dioceses where the bishop was opposed to women priests, the measure which would allow women to officiate anywhere for a limited period without reference to the bishop would bring a constant stream of women, a different one every other week, deliberately intending to defy and distress the 'anti' bishop.

Referring to the provisions set out for dissenting clergy – the £30,000 'pay-off' offered to those who would feel unable to remain in the Church – Canon Brindley described them as niggardly and deliberately stingy. 'It is our duty to press for improvement,' he wrote. 'Bad as they are, they cannot be made good, but they can be made – marginally – less bad. If a condemned prisoner is offered the choice of being shot, buried alive or burned to death, he may have little enthusiasm for any of the options, but he is still likely to choose one rather than the others.' He concluded: 'It seems to have been the intention of those who drafted this Measure that the wilderness should be as uncomfortable as possible – and consequently (we may presume) sparsely inhabited.'

Also commenting on the Financial Provisions Measure, Oswald Clark wrote that they seemed to be, not infrequently, by Scrooge (the Pensions Board) out of Skinflint (the Church Commissioners). But it would be wrong to give the impression that the AAM newsletter was concerned only with how much money their members might receive in compensation. There was also a good deal of theological reiteration as to the unacceptability of women as priests, further expression of the fear of schism both within the Church of England and with Rome and the Orthodox Churches, the latter relationship having moved much closer towards unity in recent years. In many small ways this last point can be seen to be true, with 'Romish' practices becoming more and more common in Anglican parishes. Twenty or so years ago, the very word 'priest' was, in common parlance, deemed to refer to Roman Catholics. In the Church of England there were vicars and rectors. Similarly, Anglicans went to Communion, whereas many now use the term 'Mass'. But this is just an aside. Returning to the many processes that have to be gone through before women can be priests and say the Mass, let's take another look at the second Report by the House of Bishops entitled *The Ordination of Women to the Priesthood* and published a few days before the July 1988 Synod.

This, of course, was an important document for the debate in hand, and its publication had been awaited with keen anticipation by everyone interested in the issue. In the event, it was, perhaps not unexpectedly, inconclusive, with the bishops concerned agreeing to disagree. Paragraph after paragraph began with 'disclaimers' along the lines of 'while some of us would argue', 'once more we do not agree', 'some of us then are not persuaded', and 'many of us believe this . . . others of us do not'.

More extraordinary was the considerable space given to contemplation of Adam's Rib, with questions like: 'What implication is there in the fact that woman is created from Adam's Rib?', followed by a declaration of general agreement that despite woman having been created from such a small, insignificant part of Adam's body, the argument that women are inferior to men was not accepted. Perhaps the bishops had taken account of the Rev. Esmé Beswick's theory that because woman came from Adam's side this signified her equality, but anything smaller or lower down would have constituted inferiority.

The Synod debate itself brought the wide-ranging opinion to be expected on the ordination issue, but most telling perhaps, was the Bishop of Durham's warning that the argument within the Church was promoting atheism in the world at large. He urged the Synod to press on to ordain women as soon as possible so that the boil afflicting it could be lanced, bluffs called and sufferings apportioned and brought out into the open.

Dr Jenkins argued that no church or individual could ever be certain of being right, and all had made dreadful mistakes, but he said: 'I must say plainly and decisively that the male God portrayed in and laid claim to by the arguments set out by the opponents of the ordination of women in the report we are now considering is wholly incredible. By this I mean not only that I do not believe in such a God, but that I cannot believe in such a God, and that I am clear that it is undesirable to have such a belief in God.

'This portrayal of God, however unconsciously, attempts to retain the power of men as men in the Church, is an affront to the full, vital and immensely needed humanity of women and is a denial of the mystery of God.'

Continuing his opposition to women's ordination, the Bishop of London, who was quiet in the debate, told the *Daily Telegraph* the day before:

> What I find so difficult is the fact that it is we who are constantly
> called dissenters, when it is in fact the others who are innovators
> and we believe in remaining firm to the traditional position of the
> Church of England!

If you do accept the argument that you need women priests in
order that the whole of humanity should be represented, you are
actually saying that a man alone cannot represent the whole of
humanity. That I believe to be profoundly wrong: it undermines
the incarnation. The only solution, if it is true, would be to have a
second incarnation with God as a woman.

He added that he would not leave the Church if women were to
be ordained, but would break communion with those who did
ordain women. This would lead to 'no-go' areas for women priests,
as predicted by AAM.

The Archbishop of Canterbury, in the same article, said he would
be very sad to preside over a Church with such 'no-go' areas, and
that Dr Leonard's stance seemed to suggest that a bishop who
ordained women would somehow be tainted and his other ministries
invalidated, a threat Dr Runcie found theologically indefensible.

And so to the Lambeth Conference, and the next exciting episode
in 'will they or won't they?'. It may not be part of the 'many
processes' referred to earlier in this chapter, because bishops alone
take part in the Conference, the once-a-decade gathering of Anglicans
from all corners of the world; but the Church of England cannot but
be influenced by what is happening elsewhere in the Anglican
Communion, and bishops from at least three of the provinces, New
Zealand, Canada and the USA, arrived in Canterbury at the end of
July 1988, not only seeking wholehearted acceptance of the women
they had already ordained, but elevation to the episcopate for the
chosen few.

What was most extraordinary about Lambeth 1988 was the little
time allocated to the issue of women priests. The Conference lasted
for three weeks, and yet only a single afternoon was allowed for
debate on women's ordination and just a day for women bishops.
The notion that women might one day be ordained first surfaced
nearly seventy years ago during the Lambeth Conference of 1920
and sporadically came up at subsequent gatherings until 1978, when
there was a protracted debate. By then several renegade provinces
had already begun to ordain women and the issue was whether this
would break up the worldwide Communion. It didn't, and as the

Archbishop of Canterbury said at the beginning of the first debate on women at the 1988 Conference: 'Some bishops left the conference in 1978 believing that the validity of such ordination was settled; others thought it was not. What is also clear is that no bishop present said that the ordination of women was an issue which should lead to a break in communication. Thus it would appear that diversity of practice was deemed by us to be legitimate.'

Lambeth means 'a landing place in mud', but the campus venue for Lambeth '88 at the University of Kent provided a more elevated setting on the hilltop overlooking Canterbury, and the atmosphere was far from muddy. Even so, it was easy to get lost and around every corner seemed to lurk a misdirected bishop. There were about 500 all told, plus 400 wives who convened their own get-together. In addition there were a lot of interested folk, chief among them the women wearing dog collars. One of the first I spoke to turned out to be an acknowledged frontrunner for the episcopate. She had just come from lunch and informed me that the best part of eating was smoking, something I already knew, but she seemed vaguely un-bishoply as she lit up and dropped ash on the floor.

When they weren't debating, the bishops played cricket, umpired, of course, by Dr Runcie. There was a token woman on one of the teams, but otherwise the Lambeth ladies were running the information centre and probably making the teas. Another token woman was invited to speak in the women priests debate, the first time an ordained woman had been given an official hearing. Her name was the Rev. Nan Peete, a black American, who probably played it right by talking about religion more than women's rights. She received a standing ovation for her contribution, patronage not given to the Bishop of London when he spoke in the debate.

At a press conference afterwards, he said it was an unfair question when asked whether or not Rev. Peete was a real priest. 'I am not prepared to say she is, and I'm not prepared to say she isn't,' he told reporters.

It is interesting to note that the most prominent ordained women have all been non-European. The first ever, Florence Tim Oi Li, Chinese; Nan Peete, black American; likewise, the Rt Rev. Barbara

Harris, the first Anglican bishop. Can one prejudice be so demonstrated as irrelevant in the teeth of another?

Nan Peete said: 'Growing up in the forties and fifties in a world
that rejected me and denied me my humanity based on my race, the
Church was the place I turned to for sanctuary, a place where the
priest and the people told me I was loved unconditionally as a child
of God. Yet the same church in other parts of the country also made
me feel like an outsider and not welcomed. These same feelings
come back when I am not accepted as a priest, this time because of
my sex and not my race.'

For many women who feel the same, regardless of their race,
Lambeth has become an anachronism. Monica Furlong told me: 'I
find it really outrageous to have 500 men discussing all the things
that touch women.'

Equally outraged at the possibility of women being among the
500 in 1998, WAOW, like AAM, bought four full pages of advertising
space in the church press just prior to the Canterbury gathering.
Articles published in these pages roamed from castigation of unisex
fashions to sad reflection over the sorry state of the American
Episcopal Church twelve years after the arival of women priests:

> The state of the Episcopal Church? To say the least, precarious. Its
> doctrine muddled, its order in jeopardy, it is perhaps not yet beyond
> help. Clear, unequivocal statements on the part of the bishops
> assembled at Lambeth could yet recall the American Church to its
> senses. At the very least, a firm repudiation of the expected election
> of a woman to the episcopate would warn the rest of the Anglican
> Communion not to follow the example of the Episcopal Church.
> A deranged visionary may well wander out into the desert
> believing he is charting a trail to a new promised land. Let not
> those sound of mind and spirit think of following after.

WAOW and MOW adopted very different tactics in Canterbury. While
MOW were out with their banners, WAOW were holding clandestine
sherry parties for favoured members of the press, although, during
the day-long debate on women becoming bishops – or, rather,
women becoming bishops in some provinces and not others –
WAOW leader Dr Margaret Hewitt was the only woman to speak. 'I

don't need to wear a collar to feel liberated, and neither do I need another hat,' she said.

Several Third World bishops, while siding with Dr Hewitt, seemed not to share her reasoning. One stated categorically that the male priesthood was a divine right, another that if the whole issue had grown out of the women's liberation movement it was nothing short of satanic. Such pronouncements brought groans and cries of despair from those listening.

Archbishop Desmond Tutu from South Africa said that he could not possibly discriminate against people on the basis of their gender, and that those who had not experienced the ministry of women were horribly, horribly impoverished. However, he added his concern that the consecration of a woman bishop elsewhere in the world could cause a 'kerfuffle' that would hold back the ordination of women to the priesthood in his own province.

The Bishop of Washington, John Walker, drew a comparison between women and black people, pointing out that not so long ago blacks were barred from ordination. (Interestingly, so were left-handed white men at one stage.)

Other speakers in the debate were anxious that priests ordained by a woman bishop would not be considered legitimate by some of their flock; but the overriding anxiety from all sides was that whatever happened the Anglican Communion should not break up over this or any other issue, because women becoming bishops was already a certainty before the Lambeth Conference even convened. The debate, therefore, was about division, but about not letting it really matter. The vote, as has been well publicised, resulted in a huge majority in favour of this line, although it was described to the world at large as a vote in favour of women bishops.

The essential point in all this is the different methods by which priests become bishops in the various Anglican provinces. In the Church of England, bishops are appointed, whereas elsewhere they are elected. To deny a woman priest elected to the episcopate by her diocese, would be at odds with the democratic nature of the Anglican Communion as a whole.

Of course, this democracy is seen as patchy and selective by those living in provinces where women are still denied ordination. MOW women from as far away as Australia had come to Canterbury to make this point, plaintively chorusing outside the debating hall to which they were denied access. One of them was Eileen Diesendorf, whom I had met and interviewed in Australia some months earlier. She looked tired and fed up and spoke of the continuing hardened attitude towards women. 'It's gone on for so many years,' she said bitterly.

No one was surprised by the outcome of the vote because it was not about women, only about agreement to disagree. Sister Stella Mary, whose views against the ordination of women are described in Chapter Three, came with me to Canterbury to hear the debate (relayed by closed-circuit TV from the debating hall) and she was pleased with the result.

So too was the Rev. Barbara Harris, tipped then as most likely to be the first Anglican bishop. I found her just before the result was announced, catching a quick smoke outside one of the emergency exits and easing a stiff leg caused by too much dancing. Later, after she had politely declined comment to the umpteenth press reporter, she told me that she couldn't really think beyond each step as it came, but if she became a bishop she would expect to perform and be treated as any other bishop. Suggestions bandied about by some of the Archbishops that a woman bishop might have a male bishop with her for ordinations, that she might hold office for a limited 'test' period, etc., were, quite plainly, unacceptable.

The Rev. Harris, a black American from the diocese of Massachusetts, was not at the Lambeth Conference as an interested party, but there by dint of a press pass (she edits a magazine). A former public relations consultant with an oil company, hers was a late vocation – she was forty-nine and divorced when she was ordained.

Earlier in the day, during the lunch break, I talked with outspoken sympathiser, the Bishop of Durham. What did he feel about the suggestion from some quarters that the ordination of women and consecration to the episcopate, particularly in America, was part and parcel of moral decline? 'Stupid, dishonest and a weak-minded way of going on,' was his answer. 'The typical wail of the defeated conservative.

'The arguments against women's ordination are conducted with such dogmatism, insensitivity and fear, and with apparent total incapability of seeing the psychological explanation. They will not face Freudian and Jungian thinking and say there is something in it. Those who argue against do not have an argument. It is a cry of "I am going to remain in charge."'

This is the sort of attitude Bishop Jenkins says will encourage atheism in the world at large by promoting an unbelievable God through bishops who are not credible. 'The more sophisticated and decadent Western cultures are at the leading edge and it is impracticable to go back to simple, male-dominated cultures.'

Nevertheless, he does not believe that the Church of England will have women priests by 1992–3, although he feels that the conservative upsurge may have peaked and that those 'dedicating their lives to the counsels of Canute' have limited time. 'I hope it will happen by 1992, but I don't think it will, although it is quite likely it will happen unexpectedly if Rome ordains, and Rome could do it just like that – at the stroke of a pen.'

Elaborating on the Rome issue cited by Anglicans against women's ordination, Bishop Jenkins said: 'It's a bit pathetic that people make such a fuss about not upsetting Rome. We wouldn't exist as Anglicans if we hadn't broken away; Rome still doesn't recognise our orders and shows no sign of doing so; and Rome is by no means a universally successful monolith. Recruitment to the priesthood is a problem in some places and increasingly they are using women. There is a serious possibility that Rome's hand may be forced, although I get the impression in a number of Roman circles that it is considered desirable to ordain women anyway.

'For Anglicans to hover about this issue on the grounds of upsetting Rome is a mistake. Besides, there are millions of Christians who don't belong to Rome, the Orthodox or Anglican Churches.'

So what point was the Anglican Church making at Lambeth '88? The position of women in the Church was not settled; as with the problem of polygamy, it was merely accepted that different places had different cultures, and women would become bishops in America while polygamous men converted in Africa would be allowed to keep all their wives. (Presumably this included the bishops who brought more than one to Lambeth.) In three weeks, a great deal was discussed and much of it contentious stuff over which more than five hundred men from just about every culture on earth could not possibly hope or expect to be in agreement. This, then, was the point, and there was something wonderful in that amorphous 'communion' of people who could not agree with one another yet would stay together and respect their differences. Perhaps this is the example the Church is meant to set. At any rate, it was impressive.

The MOW people didn't agree, lamenting the lack of support for women, but all the publicity over women priests throughout the summer of 1988 brought a great surge in their membership. MOW executive secretary, Margaret Orr Deas, said in October that much now rested on the re-drafted legislation for women's ordination which would be voted on in July or November 1989. Few had been happy with the original draft, with its plethora of safeguards for those 'against', but the re-worked version was expected to win an increased majority. If not, and subsequently, the vote for women was to be lost, there is the feeling that some bishops will go ahead and ordain 'illegally'. To date they have held back, preferring to wait a little longer in the hope of synodical agreement, but the Bishop of Durham has now said: 'Ordain women at any cost.' WAOW cry 'Heresy!' and 'Disgrace!', and they too, experienced a huge increase in membership during the summer months of 1988. Nobody can tell when women will become priests in the Church of England – this century, or the next – but even Margaret Orr Deas, at the heart of the 'pro' movement, says: 'We are now in for a long waiting period.'

Will it really be a *full* two thousand years?

Select bibliography

Aghiorgonssis, Maximos, *Women Priests* (Holy Cross Orthodox Press, USA, 1976)

Armstrong, Karen, *The Gospel According to Women* (Elm Tree Books, 1987)

Barr, James, *Fundamentalism* (SCM Press, 1977)

Barr, James, *Escaping from Fundamentalism* (SCM Press, 1984)

Daly, Mary, *The Church and the Second Sex* (new edn with feminist post-Christian introduction by the author) (Harper Colophon Books, 1968, 1975)

de Beauvoir, Simone, *The Second Sex* (1949) (Penguin edn ed. and transl. H. M. Parshley, 1972)

Dowell, Susan and Hurcombe, Linda, *Dispossessed Daughters of Eve* (SCM Press, 1987)

Emmanuel, Sister Vincent, *The Question of Women and the Priesthood* (Geoffrey Chapman, 1967)

Evans, Mary, *Women in the Bible* (The Paternoster Press, 1983)

Farrar, Janet and Stewart, *The Witches' Way – principles, rituals and beliefs of modern witchcraft* (Robert Hale, 1984)

Freud, Sigmund, *Totem and Taboo* (1913) (ARK edn, 1983)

Furlong, Monica, ed., *Feminine in the Church* (SPCK , 1984)

Fenwick, John, *An Evangelical's Difficulty with the Ordination of Women* (AAM publication)

Harrison, Ted, *Much Beloved Daughter* (Darton, Longman and Todd, 1985)

Hays, H. R., *The Dangerous Sex* (Methuen, 1966)

Hayter, Mary, *The New Eve in Christ: the use and abuse of the Bible in the debate about women in the Church* (SPCK, 1987)

Heeney, Brian, *The Women's Movement in the Church of England. 1850–1930* (Clarendon Press, 1988)

Honnells, John R., *The Penguin Dictionary of Religions* (1984)

Hood, Margaret, *A Laywoman's Thoughts on the Ordination of Women* (AAM publication)

Hopko, Thomas, *Women and the Priesthood* (SVS Press, 1983)

Knowles, David, *The Venerable Bede: the Ecclesiastical History of the English Nation* (731) (Dent, 1910)

Lees, Shirley, *The Role of Women*, part of 'When Christians Disagree' series ed. Oliver R. Barclay (Inter-Varsity Press, 1984)

Lofts, Nora *Women in the Old Testament* (Sampson Low, 1949)

Maitland, Sara, *A Map of the New Country: Women and Christianity* (Routledge and Kegan Paul, 1983)

Morris, Joan, *The Lady was a Bishop* (Macmillan, 1973)

Oddie, William, *What will Happen to God? Feminism and the Reconstruction of Christian Belief* (SPCK, 1984)

Radford-Ruether, Rosemary, *Sexism and God Talk* (SCM Press, 1983)

Walsh, Michael, *Roots of Christianity* (Grafton, 1986)

Walsh, James, ed., *Julian of Norwich – Revelations of Divine Love* (14–15th cent.) (Hodder and Stoughton, 1987)

Weidman, Judith L., ed., *Christian Feminism – visions of a new humanity* (Harper and Row, 1984)

Wright, Michael, *The Ordination of Women and the Doctrine of the Church* (AAM publication)

Ecclesiastical reports

The Ordination of Women to the Priesthood, consultative document presented by the Advisory Council for the Church's Ministry (1972)

The Ordination of Women to the Priesthood, second report by the House of Bishops of the General Synod of the Church of England (Central Board of Finance of the Church of England, June 1988)

Towards a Church of England response to BEM (Baptism, Eucharist and Ministry) and ARCIC (final report of the Anglican–Roman Catholic International Commission, February 1985)

Women and Holy Orders, report of a Commission appointed by the Archbishops of Canterbury and York, (CIO, 1966)

Women in Ministry: a study, report of the working party set up jointly by the Ministry Committee of the Advisory Council for the Church's Ministry and the Council for Women's Ministry in the Church (1968)

Index